CASE STUDIES IN

CULTURAL ANTHROPOLOGY

GENERAL EDITORS

George and Louise Spindler

STANFORD UNIVERSITY

THE GHOST DANCE:

Ethnohistory and Revitalization

Frontispiece: The Ghost Dance. Painting {on buckskin} by Yellow Nose, a Ute Indian who witnessed the dance among the Cheyenne.

THE GHOST DANCE:

Ethnohistory and Revitalization

ALICE BECK KEHOE

Marquette University

HOLT, RINEHART AND WINSTON

NEW YORK   CHICAGO   SAN FRANCISCO   PHILADELPHIA
MONTREAL   TORONTO   LONDON   SYDNEY   TOKYO

Cover photo: Arapaho praying during the Ghost Dance. Photographed by anthropologist James Mooney, about 1983. (Smithsonian Institution National Anthropological Archives, B.A.E. Collection)

Library of Congress Cataloging-in-Publication Data
Kehoe, Alice B., 1936–
    The ghost dance.
    (Case studies in cultural anthropology)
    Bibliography: p.
    Includes index.
    1. Ghost dance. 2. Indians of North America—Great Plains—Dances. 3. Indians of North America—Great Plains—Religion and mythology. 4. Nativistic movements—Great Plains.
    I. Title. II. Series.
E78.G73K44   1988   299'.74   88-13686

ISBN 0-03-002852-3

Requests for permission to make copies of any part of the work should be mailed to: Permissions, Holt, Rinehart and Winston, Inc., Orlando, Florida 32887.
Printed in the United States of America

8 9 0 1   016   9 8 7 6 5 4 3 2 1

Holt, Rinehart and Winston, Inc.
The Dryden Press
Saunders College Publishing

Photo Credits: Cover photo, frontispiece, figures 1, 2, 3, 4, 5, 6, 10, 11, 12, 14, 15, 16, 17, 21, 24, 32, 34—Smithsonian Institution National Anthropological Archives, B. A. E. Collection. Figures 19, 36—Smithsonian Institution National Anthropological Archives. Figure 33—Smithsonian Institution. Figures 7, 8, 9, 18, 22, 23, 25, 26, 27, 28, 29—Milwaukee Public Museum. Figure 13—courtesy of University of Nebraska Press. Figure 20—Alice Beck Kehoe. Figures 30, 31—Jo Allyn Archambault. Figure 35—The New York State Library.

Copyright Acknowledgments: The following publishers have generously given permission to use quotations from previously copyrighted works: From *The Sixth Grandfather: Black Elk's Teachings Given to John G. Heihardt*, edited and with an introduction by Raymond J. DeMallie, reprinted by permission of University of Nebraska Press. Copyright © 1984 by the University of Nebraska Press. From *Black Elk Speaks* by John G. Neihardt, copyright © John G. Neihardt Trust 1932, 1959, 1961, etc. Published by Simon & Schuster Pocket Books and The University of Nebraska Press. From *Blood on the Land* by Rex Wyler, by permission of Everest House/Dodd, Mead & Company, Inc. From *Voices from Wounded Knee*, by permission of Akwesasne Notes, Mohawk Nation, Rooseveltown, N.Y. From *Airlift to Wounded Knee* by Bill Zimmerman, reprinted with the permission of The Ohio University Press, Athens.

Foreword

ABOUT THE SERIES

These case studies in cultural anthropology are designed to bring to students, in beginning and intermediate courses in the social sciences, insights into the richness and complexity of human life as it is lived in different places. They are written by men and women who have lived in the societies they write about and who are professionally trained as observers and interpreters of human behavior. The authors are also teachers, and in writing their books they have kept the students who will read them foremost in their minds. We believe that when an understanding of ways of life very different from one's own is gained, abstractions and generalizations about social structure, cultural values, subsistence techniques, and the other universal categories of human social behavior become meaningful.

ABOUT THE AUTHOR

Alice Beck Kehoe was born in New York City on September 18, 1934 and grew up in the suburbs of Washington, D.C., and New York. In junior high school, she became interested in anthropology and archaeology, and her first employment, during the summer she was sixteen, was as a clerk-typist in the American Museum of Natural History's Department of Anthropology. She worked at the Museum again the next summer, assisting curators in a variety of tasks, and for the next four years as a student assistant while studying anthropology at Barnard College in New York. Graduating from Barnard in 1956, Kehoe went to Browning, Montana, on the Blackfeet Reservation as assistant at the Museum of the Plains Indian. She married the young director of the Museum, Thomas F. Kehoe, and the following year, after he had completed his master's thesis at the University of Washington, they both enrolled in the Ph.D. program at Harvard University.

In 1959, Thomas Kehoe was appointed first Provincial Archaeologist for the province of Saskatchewan in central Canada. The Kehoes moved to Regina, and Alice assisted Thomas in his archaeological research. By 1961, the Kehoes were ready to submit proposals for their doctoral dissertations to the faculty at Harvard. Thomas proposed to excavate the major prehistoric site of Gull Lake in southwestern Saskatchewan; Alice, to excavate the first successful fur trade post, in east-central Saskatchewan. Her proposal was rejected on the grounds that she had to do work independent of her husband—not just several hundred miles distant, but outside the field of archaeology. Alice was thus forced to change the focus of her graduate study from archaeology to ethnology, and she began to search for a suitable topic of research among the Indians of Saskatchewan. By the fortunate circumstances she describes in Chapter 10, she discovered that the Ghost Dance religion taught by the Paiute prophet Jack Wilson had been accepted by one small community of Dakota outside Prince Albert, Saskatchewan. This New Tidings religion became the topic of Kehoe's doctoral dissertation, which was completed in 1964.

Kehoe published a summary of her research in the scholarly journal *Plains Anthropologist*, anticipating it would cause a stir among anthropologists, many of whom accepted the sociologist Bernard Barber's 1941 claim that the Ghost Dance religion had died in the Wounded Knee Massacre in 1890. Few seemed to see the new research as a challenge to existing theory, and Kehoe became interested in critically examining social science to understand why some theories become popular.

Since 1968 (after teaching for three years at the University of Nebraska), Kehoe has been a professor of anthropology at Marquette University, teaching three undergraduate courses every semester. She has continued both ethnographic and archaeological research on Northwestern Plains Indians and also publishes critiques of anthropological theory. Her 1981 textbook, *North American Indians: A Comprehensive Account*, is widely used. One focus of Kehoe's work has been to view American Indians not as examples or models of supposed evolutionary stages or types, but as people engaged in the universal struggle for life, liberty, and the pursuit of happiness.

THIS CASE STUDY

This case study is a departure from the format established for the series. It is not a descriptive analysis of an entire way of life but rather a focused analysis of some aspect of it. In this case the focus is the Ghost Dance and other related messianic movements that were a most significant aspect of American Indian life during the closing phases of the nineteenth century and the beginning decades of the twentieth.

The Ghost Dance and its companion movements still reverberate today in Native American communities. In our own fieldwork with the Menominee, and through their network, with Chippewa, Winnebago, and Potowatami, we encountered the Dream Dance and the Peyote Church. Both of these religions are today's expressions of movements similar in many respects to the Ghost Dance and in some ways affected directly by it. Though in their present form these religions are institutionalized and stable, they include in their ideologies much that reflects the adaptations made by Native American populations in order to survive in the face of the forces of destruction that swept through the Plains in the final spasms of occupation and exploitation by whites.

Alice Kehoe has devoted her professional life to the study of Native American peoples and their cultures. Not long ago most American anthropologists did fieldwork with American Indians. In fact, American anthropology is in many respects a child of Native America. True, at times the stepchild has been rejected, in fact disowned by its parents, but the relationship cannot be denied. Many characteristics of our field are traceable to this relationship.

Today most young anthropologists do their fieldwork abroad, or, paradoxically, in the United States, but not with Indians. This is not because the work is finished. Native Americans are as active as ever as they continue the never-ending battle to preserve their identity and at the same time live and work in a complex, dynamic, modern society that is in many respects antithetical to Native American world views and that still labors with the burden of racism. But the "anthros" have mostly gone away, at least as students of American Indian life. They have come back, in some cases, as helpers.

Alice Kehoe, like us, came into anthropology when there was still a deep commitment to understanding the multifaceted native American cultures that once dominated the landscape of North America, and their adaptations to the disastrous impact of our culture, politics, and economy upon them. We have always hoped that this understanding could help make Indian–white relations better and even influence governmental policy.

This case study is a contribution in that direction. It is divided into two parts. The first is a fascinating account of the Ghost Dance and related events and personages. The second is a survey of attempts by social scientists, including anthropologists, to develop appropriate theory for the analysis of such processes. Some readers may find one part more interesting or useful than the other, but together they represent a balanced and serious attempt to understand the Ghost Dance as a reaction to conquest, defeat, and deprivation. This balance should be particularly important to student readers.

GEORGE AND LOUISE SPINDLER
Series Editors
Calistoga, California

In Deep Appreciation:
Robert Goodvoice
Florence and Joe Douquette
Sam Buffalo

Preface

On the first day of January 1889, a man in Nevada received a commission from God. People were pushing each other around, competing for resources they should be sharing. God appointed the man in Nevada to tell all the people to put away the things of war, to stop their quarrels, to work, to be good, to love one another, to dance in great circles together. People in Nevada, and for many thousands of miles beyond, eagerly listened to this gospel message. Pilgrims came by the hundreds to sit at the prophet's feet. Some came as skeptics: They usually left impressed by the prophet's power. By the summer of 1890, many described the prophet as a Christ; there were others who suspected the preaching of the gospel was a cover for plotting rebellion against the United States government. When, in December 1890, first the famous chief Sitting Bull and then a couple hundred other Sioux Indians, including women and children, were killed by United States officers, citizens in the eastern United States demanded to know whether there was in fact a plotted rebellion, or were the Indians victims of incompetent, trigger-happy agents and soldiers.

Out of the investigations of an experienced anthropologist, James Mooney, came the answer, not as a simple report but as a thick study in American Indian history—ethnohistory—and in comparative religions. Mooney's classic monograph is a landmark of anthropological research and a model. Above all, it forces readers to understand that American Indians are humans whose motives are as complex, and whose actions and events are as complicated, as those of any other group of persons in our world. Mooney gives no simple answers or pseudoscientific explanations. He presents instead a wonderfully rich description of many historical happenings and many religions, Christianity included. The thoughtful reader is rewarded by the kind of knowledge we find in the greatest works of literature, a deepening of our understanding of what it is to be human.

In the first part of this book, I put Mooney's study of the Nevada prophet, Jack Wilson, and the tragic killings of 1890 in two perspectives. First, I present Mooney's findings on the events in Nevada in 1889. This is followed by fuller descriptions of the culture of the prophet, who was a Paiute Indian, and of the Lakota Sioux sufferings that culminated in the massacre that outraged the civilized world. To contrast with this well-known event, I describe a small community of Sioux in Canada, once refugees from the Minnesota Indian wars, who accepted Jack Wilson's gospel and practiced it into the 1960s. Then we go to a twentieth-century Lakota evangelist, Nick Black Elk, who has become a prophet for thousands of Americans and Europeans today seeking religious guidance. The last chapter in Part 1 chronicles the 1973 revolt of Indians against the United States government, taking place at the site of the 1890 massacre. American Indians are very much part of the contemporary United States.

The second part of this book concerns efforts to analyze historical events such as those described in the preceding chapters. We want to figure out why people behave as they have, what they are likely to do, what we can do to secure our personal goals. Can we predict human behavior? Can we influence events? Our society hopes we are in the process of discovering cause-and-effect relationships that will enable us to improve our society. Social scientists are employed to come up with observations, codify them, and manipulate them to test possible links betraying cause and effect. What many citizens do not realize is that social scientists' conclusions are used to develop and justify social policies that affect millions of us. We had better know something about social science, because it claims to know something about us, and what it claims to know becomes part of the ongoing regulation of our lives.

Anthropologists are one kind of social scientist, the kind that insists that comparing different societies—their beliefs and ways of life—can be the key to a better understanding of ourselves as well as others. Part 2 of this book brings in anthropologists' studies of other American Indian societies and the explanations of events derived from these studies. I show how anthropologists produce models of behavior from observations. The model developed by the contemporary anthropologist Anthony F. C. Wallace from his study of another Indian prophet, the New York Iroquois Handsome Lake, seems to fit many cases, including that of Jack Wilson, the Paiute in Nevada. Wallace focused on religious change, but his model also describes how political beliefs and organization, economic systems, and social customs change. From what seems like an esoteric topic, Indian prophets of a century or two ago, anthropologists have drawn models of human behavior that give insight into contemporary events of American life, from superpower summit meetings to the successes, and fading out, of rock music groups.

This book could have used examples more familiar to most American students than American Indian religious and political events. It could have used the Grateful Dead and its prophet Jerry Garcia, or Bob Dylan, or Bruce Springsteen. It uses, instead, Jack Wilson and Handsome Lake and Black Elk and the AIM leaders of the 1970s, not because anthropologists study only exotic peoples, but because we cannot ignore these Americans, whose ancestors watched Columbus step on the shore of a continent discovered many thousands of years earlier. By using examples from American Indian history, up to the recent events of the 1970s, this book will add to students' knowledge of present-day America. These examples are not exotic: They are of fellow Americans, and of their efforts to live decent lives in their native country.

Acknowledgments

This book exists only because Joe and Florence Douquette, Robert Good-voice, and Henry Two Bears trusted me to honor that which is *wakan*. My debt to them goes far beyond gratitude for data that earned me my graduate degree; their examples of leading clean, honest lives in the face of unending adversities are inspirational.

The research, dating 1961–1964, used in this book was materially assisted by Mabel Richards; Piakwutch, Arthur Brown, and Winona Frank of Pound-maker's and Little Pine Reserves; Hector Obey and, in 1973, Max and Wayne Goodwill of Standing Buffalo Reserve; Charlie Red Hawk of Moose Woods (White Cap) Reserve; and Allan R. Turner, then Provincial Archivist of Saskatchewan. In 1973, I returned to Round Plain and talked with Sam Buffalo. In 1984, I went back to ask permission to use the material in this book. With Mr. Two Bears deceased since 1965, Robert Goodvoice and Sam Buffalo both incapacitated by the afflictions of old age, and the Douquettes having moved to Joe's Cree reserve, I talked with Band Chief Cy Standing of Sioux Wahpeton, who agreed that it no longer seemed necessary to keep the information on New Tidings confidential.

George and Louise Spindler remained interested in this material over many years of developing the case studies series, and I am most grateful to them for this sustained consideration and for their support once the publisher agreed to this deviation from the standard format of the series. Gale Miller of Marquette University has been most helpful in developing the chapters on social science. Adrian Heidenreich generously gave me a copy of his master's thesis on the Ghost Dance, James Howard showed me a copy of his mono-graph on the Canadian Dakota several years before it was published, and Michael Hittman discussed his research on Mason Valley before his disser-tation became available. JoAllyn Archambault of the Department of An-thropology, Smithsonian Institution, has been invaluable in critically reading the sections on the Lakota—extending a guiding hand through the morass of polemics on AIM—though I alone take responsibility for my statements. The comments of manuscript reviewers John Moore and Alan Marshall were helpful in focusing the structure of the book.

I also thank my professors at Harvard, J. O. Brew who pushed me into ethnography, and Evon Z. Vogt who was the best dissertation chair any student could want. It is true that I resented, at the time, Jo's extreme caution in developing my dissertation topic, but I now am truly grateful to him for opening a new road for my life. It helps, too, that once I had that degree in hand, in 1964, I did excavate the site of François' House.

Finally, as always, I acknowledge my husband's partnership, and our sons' good-humored forbearance in all our projects.

Contents

Illustrations

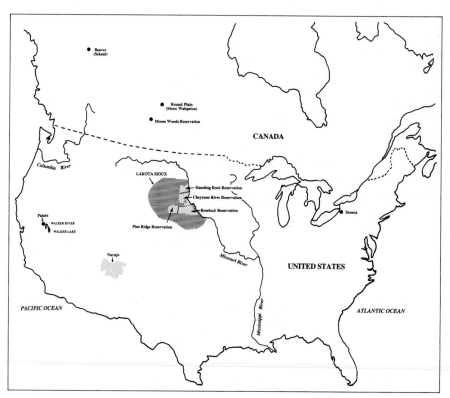

Map: Locations of North American Indian peoples described in this book.

PART ONE | Ethnohistory

Figure 1. Jack Wilson (Wovoka). Photographed in Mason Valley, Nevada, by anthropologist James Mooney, 1891.

1/The Ghost Dance Religion

New Year's Day, 1892. Nevada.

A wagon jounces over a maze of cattle trails crisscrossing a snowy valley floor. In the wagon, James Mooney, from the Smithsonian Institution in faraway Washington, D.C., is looking for the Indian messiah, Wovoka, blamed for riling up the Sioux, nearly three hundred of whom now lie buried by Wounded Knee Creek in South Dakota. The men in the wagon see a man with a gun over his shoulder walking in the distance.

"I believe that's Jack now!" exclaims one of Mooney's guides. "Jack Wilson," he calls to the messiah, whose Paiute name is Wovoka. Mooney's other guide, Charley Sheep, Wovoka's uncle, shouts to his nephew in the Paiute language. The hunter comes over to the wagon.

"I saw that he was a young man," Mooney recorded, "a dark full-blood, compactly built, and taller than the Paiute generally, being nearly 6 feet in height. He was well dressed in white man's clothes, with the broad-brimmed white felt hat common in the west, secured on his head by means of a beaded ribbon under the chin. . . . He wore a good pair of boots. His hair was cut off square on a line below the base of the ears, after the manner of his tribe. His countenance was open and expressive of firmness and decision" (Mooney [1896] 1973:768–769).

That evening, James Mooney formally interviewed Jack Wilson in his home, a circular lodge ten feet in diameter, built of bundles of tule reeds tied to a pole frame. In the middle of the lodge, a bright fire of sagebrush stalks sent sparks flying out of the wide smoke hole. Several other Paiutes were with Jack, his wife, baby, and little son when Mooney arrived with a guide and an interpreter. Mooney noticed that although all the Paiutes dressed in "white man's" clothes, they preferred to live in traditional wickiups. Only Paiute baskets furnished Jack Wilson's home; no beds, no storage trunks, no pots or pans, nothing of alien manufacture except the hunting gun and knife lay in the wickiup, though the family could have bought the invaders' goods. Jack had steady employment as a ranch laborer, and from his wages he could have constructed a cabin and lived in it, sitting on chairs and eating bread and beef from metal utensils. Instead, Jack and Mary, his wife, wanted to follow the ways of their people as well as they could in a valley overrun with Euro-American settlement. The couple hunted, fished, and gathered pine nuts and other seeds and wild plants. They practiced their Paiute religion

3

rather than the Presbyterian Christianity Jack's employer insisted on teaching them. Mooney was forced to bring a Euro-American settler, Edward Dyer, to interpret for him because Jack would speak only his native Paiute, though he had some familiarity with English. This was Mason Valley, in the heart of Paiute territory, and for Jack and Mary it was still Paiute.

Jack Wilson told Mooney that he had been born four years before the well-remembered battle between Paiutes and American invaders at Pyramid Lake. The battle had been touched off by miners seizing two Paiute women. The men of the Paiute community managed to rescue the two women. No harm was done to the miners, but they claimed they were victims of an "Indian outrage," raised a large party of their fellows, and set off to massacre the Paiutes. Expecting trouble, the Paiute men ambushed the mob of miners at a narrow pass, and although armed mostly with only bows and arrows, killed nearly fifty of the mob, routing the rest and saving the families in the Indian camp. Jack Wilson's father, Tavibo, was a leader of the Paiute community at that time. He was recognized as spiritually blessed—gifted and trained to communicate with invisible powers. By means of this gift, carefully cultivated, Tavibo was said to be able to control the weather.

Tavibo left the community when his son Wovoka was in his early teens, and the boy was taken on by David Wilson, a Euro-American rancher with sons of his own close in age to the Paiute youth. Though employed as a ranch hand, Wovoka was strongly encouraged to join the Wilson family in daily prayers and Bible reading, and Jack, as he came to be called, became good friends with the Wilson boys. Through these years with the Wilsons, Jack's loyalty to, and pride in, his own Paiute people never wavered. When he was about twenty, he married a Paiute woman who shared his commitment to the Paiute way of life. With his wages from the ranch, Jack and Mary bought the

Figure 2.   A Tövusi-dökadö Pauite family by its wickiup. Photographed by anthropologist James Mooney in Mason Valley, Nevada, January 1892.

hunting gun and ammunition, good-quality "white man's" clothes, and ornaments suited to their dignity as a respected younger couple in the Mason Valley community.

As a young adult, Jack Wilson began to develop a reputation as a weather doctor like his father. Paiute believe that a young person lacks the maturity and inner strength to function as a spiritual agent, but Jack was showing the self-discipline, sound judgment, and concern for others that marked Indians gifted as doctors in the native tradition. Jack led the circle dances through which Paiute opened themselves to spiritual influence. Moving always along the path of the sun—clockwise to the left—men, women, and children joined hands in a symbol of the community's living through the circle of the days. As they danced they listened to Jack Wilson's songs celebrating the Almighty and Its wondrous manifestations: the mountains, the clouds, snow, stars, trees, antelope. Between dances, the people sat at Jack's feet, listening to him preach faith in universal love.

The climax of Jack's personal growth came during a dramatic total eclipse of the sun on January 1, 1889. He was lying in his wickiup very ill with a fever. Paiute around him saw the sky darkening although it was midday. Some monstrous force was overcoming the sun! People shot off guns at the apparition, they yelled, some wailed as at a death. Jack Wilson felt himself losing consciousness. It seemed to him he was taken up to heaven and brought before God. God gave him a message to the people of earth, a gospel of peace and right living. Then he and the sun regained their normal life.

Jack Wilson was now a prophet. Tall, handsome, with a commanding presence, Jack already was respected for his weather control power. (The unusual snow blanketing Mason Valley when James Mooney visited was said to be Jack's doing.) Confidence in his God-given mission further enhanced Jack Wilson's reputation. Indians came from other districts to hear him, and even Mormon settlers in Nevada joined his audiences. To carry out his mission, Jack Wilson went to the regional Indian agency at Pyramid Lake and asked one of the employees to prepare and mail a letter to the President of the United States, explaining the Paiute doctor's holy mission and suggesting that if the United States government would send him a small regular salary, he would convey God's message to all the people of Nevada and, into the bargain, make it rain whenever they wished. The agency employee never sent the letter. It was agency policy to "silently ignore" Indians' efforts toward "notoriety." The agent would not even deign to meet the prophet.

Jack Wilson did not need the support of officials. His deep sincerity and utter conviction of his mission quickly persuaded every open-minded hearer of its importance. Indians came on pilgrimages to Mason Valley, some out of curiosity, others seeking guidance and healing in that time of afflictions besetting their peoples. Mormons came too, debating whether Jack Wilson was the fulfillment of a prophecy of their founder, Joseph Smith, Jr., that the Messiah would appear in human form in 1890. Jack Wilson himself consistently explained that he was *a* messiah *like* Jesus but not the Christ of the

Christians. Both Indians and Euro-Americans tended to ignore Jack's pro-
testations and to identify him as "the Christ." Word spread that the Son of
God was preaching in western Nevada.

Throughout 1889 and 1890, railroads carried delegates from a number of
Indian nations east of the Rockies to investigate the messiah in Mason Valley.
Visitors found ceremonial grounds maintained beside the Paiute settlements,
flat cleared areas with low willow-frame shelters around the open dancing
space. Paiutes gathered periodically to dance and pray for four days and
nights, ending on the fifth morning shaking their blankets and shawls to
symbolize driving out evil. In Mason Valley itself, Jack Wilson would attend
the dances, repeating his holy message and, from time to time, trembling and
passing into a trance to confirm the revelations. Delegates from other reservations were sent back home with tokens of Jack Wilson's holy power:
bricks of ground red ocher dug from Mount Grant south of Mason Valley,
the Mount Sinai of Northern Paiute religion; the strikingly marked feathers
of the magpie; pine nuts, the "daily bread" of the Paiutes; and robes of woven
strips of rabbit fur, the Paiutes' traditional covering. James Mooney's respectful interest in the prophet's teachings earned him the privilege of carrying
such tokens to his friends on the Cheyenne and Arapaho reservations east
of the mountains.

Jack Wilson told Mooney that when "the sun died" that winter day in
1889 and, dying with it, he was taken up to heaven,

> he saw God, with all the people who had died long ago engaged in their oldtime
> sports and occupations, all happy and forever young. It was a pleasant land and
> full of game. After showing him all, God told him he must go back and tell his
> people they must be good and love one another, have no quarreling, and live in
> peace with the whites; that they must work, and not lie or steal; that they must
> put away all the old practices that savored of war; that if they faithfully obeyed
> his instructions they would at last be reunited with their friends in this other world,
> where there would be no more death or sickness or old age. He was then given
> the dance which he was commanded to bring back to his people. By performing
> this dance at intervals, for five consecutive days each time, they would secure this
> happiness to themselves and hasten the event. Finally God gave him control over
> the elements so that he could make it rain or snow or be dry at will, and appointed
> him his deputy to take charge of affairs in the west, while "Governor Harrison"
> [President of the United States at the time] would attend to matters in the east,
> and he, God, would look after the world above. He then returned to earth and
> began to preach as he was directed, convincing the people by exercising the won-
> derful powers that had been given him. (Mooney [1896] 1973:771–772)

Before Mooney's visit, Jack Wilson had repeated his gospel, in August
1891, to a literate young Arapaho man who had journeyed with other Arapaho
and Cheyenne to discover the truth about this fabled messiah. Jack instructed
his visitors, according to the Arapaho's notes:

> When you get home you make dance, and will give you the same. . . . He likes
> you folk, you give him good, many things, he heart been sitting feel good. After
> you get home, will give good cloud, and give you chance to make you feel good.

and he give you good spirit. and he give you all a good paint. . . .

Grandfather said when he die never no cry. no hurt anybody. no fight, good behave always, it will give you satisfaction, this young man, he is a good Father and mother, dont tell no white man. Jueses [Jesus?] was on ground, he just like cloud. Everybody is alive agin, I dont know when they will [be] here, may be this fall or in spring.

Everybody never get sick, be young again,—(if young fellow no sick any more,) work for white men never trouble with him until you leave, when it shake the earth dont be afraid no harm any body.

You make dance for six weeks night, and put you foot [food?] in dance to eat for every body and wash in the water. that is all to tell, I am in to you. and you will received a good words from him some time, Dont tell lie. (Mooney [1896] 1973:780–781)

Seeing the red ocher paint, the magpie feathers, the pine nuts, and the rabbit skin robes from the messiah, his Arapaho friends shared this message with James Mooney. Jack Wilson himself had trusted this white man. Thanks to this Arapaho document, we know that Jack Wilson himself obeyed his injunction, "Dont tell lie": he had confided to the Smithsonian anthropologist the same gospel he brought to his Indian disciples.

"A clean, honest life" is the core of Jack Wilson's guidance, summed up seventy years later by a Dakota Sioux who had grown up in the Ghost Dance religion. The circling dance of the congregations following Jack Wilson's gospel symbolized the ingathering of all people in the embrace of Our Father, God, and in his earthly deputy Jack Wilson. As the people move in harmony in the dance around the path of the sun, leftward, so they must live and work in harmony. Jack Wilson was convinced that if every Indian would dance this belief, the great expression of faith and love would sweep evil from the earth, renewing its goodness in every form, from youth and health to abundant food.

This was a complete religion. It had a transcendental origin in the prophet's visit to God, and a continuing power rooted in the eternal Father. Its message of earthly renewal was universalistic, although Jack Wilson felt it was useless to preach it to those Euro-Americans who were heedlessly persecuting the Indian peoples. That Jack shared his gospel with those non-Indians who came to him as pilgrims demonstrates that it was basically applicable to all people of goodwill. The gospel outlined personal behavior and provided the means to unite individuals into congregations to help one another. Its principal ceremony, the circling dance, pleased and satisfied the senses of the participants, and through the trances easily induced during the long ritual, it offered opportunities to experience profound emotional catharsis. Men and women, persons of all ages and capabilities, were welcomed into a faith of hope for the future, consolation and assistance in the present, and honor to the Indians who had passed into the afterlife. It was a marvelous message for people suffering, as the Indians of the West were in 1889, terrible epidemics; loss of their lands, their economic resources, and their political autonomy; malnourishment and wretched housing; and a campaign of cultural genocide aimed at eradicating their languages, their customs, and their beliefs.

Jack Wilson's religion was immediately taken up by his own people, the Northern Paiute, by other Paiute groups, by the Utes, the Shoshoni, and the Washo in western Nevada. It was carried westward across the Sierra Nevada and espoused by many of the Indians of California. To the south, the religion was accepted by the western Arizona Mohave, Cohonino, and Pai, but not by most other peoples of the American Southwest. East of the Rockies, the religion spread through the Shoshoni and Arapaho in Wyoming to other Arapaho, Cheyenne, Assiniboin, Gros Ventre (Atsina), Mandan, Arikara, Pawnee, Caddo, Kichai, Wichita, Kiowa, Kiowa-Apache, Comanche, Delaware (living by this time in Oklahoma), Oto, and the western Sioux, especially the Teton bands. The mechanism by which this religion spread was usually a person visiting another tribe, observing the new ceremonial dance and becoming inspired by its gospel, and returning home to urge relatives and friends to try the new faith. Leaders of these evangelists' communities would often appoint respected persons to travel to Nevada to investigate this claim of a new messiah. The delegates frequently returned as converts, testifying to the truth of the faith and firing the enthusiasm of their communities. Those who remained skeptics did not always succeed in defusing the flame of faith in others.

Never an organized church, Jack Wilson's religion thus spread by independent converts from California through Oklahoma. Not all the communities who took it up continued to practice it, when months or years passed without the hoped-for earth renewal. Much of Jack Wilson's religion has persisted, however, and has been incorporated into the regular religious life of Indian groups, especially on Oklahoma reservations. To merge into a complex of beliefs and rituals rather than be an exclusive religion was entirely in accordance with Jack Wilson's respect for traditional Indian religions, which he saw reinforced, not supplanted, by his revelations. Though the Sioux generally dropped the Ghost Dance religion after their military defeats following their initial acceptance of the ritual, older people among the Sioux could be heard occasionally singing Ghost Dance songs in the 1930s. The last real congregation of adherents to Jack Wilson's gospel continued to worship together into the 1960s, and at least one who survived into the 1980s never abandoned the faith. There were sporadic attempts to revive the Ghost Dance religion in the 1970s, though these failed to kindle the enthusiasm met by the original proselytizers.

"Ghost Dance" is the name usually applied to Jack Wilson's religion, because the prophet foresaw the resurrection of the recently dead with the hoped-for renewal of the earth. Paiute themselves simply called their practice of the faith "dance in a circle," Shoshoni called it "everybody dragging" (speaking of people pulling others along as they circled), Comanche called it "the Father's Dance," Kiowa, "dance with clasped hands," and Caddo, "prayer of all to the Father" or "my [Father's] children's dance." The Sioux and Arapaho did use the term "spirit [ghost] dance," and the English name seems to have come from translation of the Sioux. The last active congregation, however, referred to their religion as the New Tidings, stressing its parallel to Jesus' gospel.

Figure 3. Arapaho praying during the Ghost Dance. Photographed by anthropologist James Mooney, about 1893.

To his last days in 1932, Jack Wilson served as Father to believers. He counseled them, in person and by letters, and he gave them holy red ocher paint, symbolizing life, packed into rinsed-out tomato cans (the red labels indicated the contents). With his followers, he was saddened that not enough Indians danced the new faith to create the surge of spiritual power that could have renewed the earth, but resurrection was only a hope. The heart of his religion was his creed, the knowledge that a "clean, honest life" is the only good life.

WHAT'S THIS ALL ABOUT?

James Mooney's task, in 1891, was simply to investigate what was in back of the tragic death of so many Sioux people camped at Wounded Knee Creek in December 1890. Did the Sioux really plan to battle the United States

Figure 4. Arapaho Ghost Dance, 1891. Photographed by anthropologist James Mooney.

forces? Was the mysterious new cult, the "Ghost Dance," stimulating the Indians to such crazy, dangerous behavior? The government wanted to know, American colonists settling in the western Plains wanted to know, the American public in the eastern cities—concerned that undisciplined soldiers might be wantonly killing helpless, conquered Indians—wanted to know.

Mooney's first employment, as a young man, had been as a journalist, and he used the skills of a journalist in his investigation. But Mooney had from his teens been fascinated by the Indians who had preceded his own people in America. He gave up journalism to work in the Smithsonian Institution's Bureau of American Ethnology, traveling to Indian communities to record their cultures. He was impelled by a powerful desire to understand human behavior, and he became one of the first generation of professional anthropologists because he was convinced that to understand human behavior, we must see it and compare it in many societies. His researches were designed to give us these comparative data.

The result of Mooney's investigation in 1891 and 1892 was a long, detailed report presenting not only a full account of Jack Wilson's beliefs, the spread of his doctrine to hundreds of Indian groups, and the events leading to the Wounded Knee deaths, but also many chapters describing other nineteenth-century American Indian prophets, and prophets in Western and Asian traditions. From these comparisons, we might come to understand how, and why, religions arise.

A century after Mooney's wagon ride to the little wickiup in the snowy valley in Nevada, his questions on the how and why of religions are more important than ever. In our time, we see the quest of millions of people for spiritual guidance and meaning in their lives. We see, also, religious fanaticism apparently driving modern nations to terrorism and wars. Is it possible that the story of an obscure Paiute man in Nevada a hundred years ago might help us fashion more satisfying lives for ourselves and our fellow citizens?

Anthropologists' experience indicates that well-described case histories compared with one another can illuminate basic human behavior. We are all members of the same species, with similar physical and emotional needs. This principle underlying anthropological research makes Jack Wilson's story potentially valuable for contemporary understanding, for Mooney's exhaustive on-the-spot investigations have given us one of the richest case histories ever recorded. Subsequent anthropologists have amplified it with ethnohistorical (that is, history of a particular ethnic group) research on the Paiute and the peoples of the Plateau region of northwestern America (see Chapter 7); with analyses aimed at pinpointing causal factors in religious or societal change (see Chapter 8); and with studies drawing a model of religious and societal change out of rich descriptions (see Chapter 9). The model technically termed "revitalization" drawn by the contemporary anthropologist Anthony F. C. Wallace seems to clarify what happened a hundred years ago in Nevada and among the Sioux, and, more important, illuminates what is happening today within and outside America.

This book is constructed in two parts. The first, Chapters 1 through 6, are primarily ethnohistorical in emphasizing description of American Indians from Jack Wilson and his Paiute people, to the contemporary Lakota Sioux culture and communities. These chapters make it clear that most American Indian peoples are still very much alive, through strength of will, faith, and intelligent adaptation to circumstances as these changed. The second part of the book is more social-scientific in focus, though it includes much ethnohistorical data. In this part, the most popular social-science explanations of the Ghost Dance are presented and evaluated. The aim of these chapters is to show how social scientists (sociologists as well as anthropologists) collect, select, and analyze data. It will be apparent that social science differs in several fundamental features from the physical sciences. It will also be apparent that unexamined prejudices or biases have sometimes influenced social scientists to misrepresent historical facts; this has become more visible as we reject the traditional assumption in Western societies of superiority to all other cultures.

The final chapter tells the reader a personal history: Books do not happen in a vacuum, and the chapter shows how *this* author came to write *this particular* book. Being detoured, by a common form of discrimination, from the narrow path of a career planned in college brought the author to discover a congregation that cast a light on the Ghost Dance religion quite different from the stereotype found in textbooks. That night in a log cabin in the Saskatchewan pine forest molded the young anthropologist's life. The people in the cabin that night—old Mr. Two Bears, now deceased; Robert Goodvoice; Florence and Joe Douquette—would wish, with the author, that reading this book will help you understand the situation of Indian people today, and your own struggle to lead a "clean, honest life."

2/Massacre at Wounded Knee Creek

Jack Wilson was a prophet of peace. Like Jesus, he was both model and teacher of pacifism. His gospel, like Jesus', spread far beyond his native land, carried by men often of languages and cultural traditions different from his own. Jack Wilson's professed disciples, like those following Jesus, in time came to include persons who failed to grasp the central importance of peace in the gospel. The Roman emperor Constantine took the monogram of Christ for a magic sign to bring him victory in battle; the Teton Sioux (Lakota) leader Kicking Bear, in the spring of 1890, introduced to his fellow western Sioux a special shirt about which he claimed, "The bullets will not go through these shirts and dresses, so they all have these dresses for war" (Mooney [1896] 1973:798). A Prince of Peace was again betrayed.

"Ghost shirts" became the touchstone for seeing belligerent rebellion in the Ghost Dance religion. Kicking Bear had seen Arapaho "paint the white muslins they made holy shirts and dresses out of with blue across the back, and alongside of this is a line of yellow paint. They also paint in the front part of the shirts and dresses. A picture of an eagle is made on the back of all the shirts and dresses. On the shoulders and on the sleeves they tied eagle feathers" (Mooney [1896] 1973:798). James Mooney suggested that the Arapaho with whom Kicking Bear had danced may have copied the idea of holy dresses from Mormons who used an "endowment robe" of white muslin ornamented with symbols of their faith. Many Mormons of Mooney's time believed that wearing these dresses protected them from dangers, including bullets. Some Mormons joined their Indian neighbors in the new messiah's dance, and they may have been wearing their robes. Some Paiutes, Shoshoni, and other Indians joined the Mormon church and may have owned and worn "endowment robes" when they later participated in Jack Wilson's ritual. A band of Shoshoni share a Wyoming reservation with an Arapaho band, and these Arapaho may have come across the holy dress through Shoshoni contacts or perhaps when visiting across the Rockies in Nevada.

Whether or not Kicking Bear invented the notion of magic bulletproof shirts for Ghost Dance followers, he was responsible for introducing it to the Sioux and allowing it to distort the true Ghost Dance religion. By early 1891, the Southern Arapaho sharing territory with the Cheyenne in Oklahoma agreed with the Cheyenne that wearing a special costume for the Dance smelled too strongly of Sioux belligerency and tainted the holy gospel. The

Oklahoma Arapaho repudiated their Wyoming cousins' "ghost shirts." Jack Wilson would have been pleased at their action, for when he learned of the Sioux claims for their ghost shirts, he insisted they had no place in his doctrine. He was a prophet, though, not a pope, and he could not stop distant people from deforming his revelations.

On May 29, 1890, a Mr. Charles L. Hyde of Pierre, South Dakota, wrote to the Secretary of the Interior in Washington that he had learned the Sioux were planning a rebellion. Hyde had apparently been talking with a youth from Pine Ridge Reservation whose relatives had written to him, at school in Pierre, of the excitement at home over the news of the messiah. The Secretary of the Interior passed the letter on to the Commissioner of the Bureau of Indian Affairs, who sent copies to the agents of the several Sioux reservations, asking them to check into the matter. None of the agents found reason to be disturbed, although they considered the Indians' "craziness" over the "messiah dance" annoying. Most of the agents had been recently appointed as rewards for their political support of President Harrison and his party. They were generally poorly acquainted with the people they were to administer, and unlikely to be critical of the President's orders toward Indians.

President Harrison's government had promulgated, in 1889, a new Indian policy, not radically different from preceding policy except in the urgency expressed in its first clause:

> First, the anomalous position heretofore occupied by the Indians in this country can no longer be maintained.
>
> Second, the logic of events demands the absorption of the Indians into our national life not as Indians but as American citizens.
>
> Third, as soon as wise conservation will permit it, the relations of the Indians to the government must rest solely upon the recognition of their individuality [that is, the Indians must be legally private persons, not subordinate to the tribe as a corporate entity].
>
> Fourth, the individual must conform to the white man's ways, peaceably if they will, forcibly if they must.
>
> Fifth, compulsory education.
>
> Sixth, tribal relationship should be broken.
>
> Seventh, honest administration.
>
> Eighth, competent and honest servants of the government. (quoted in Milligan 1976:121)

Why the urgency in this policy? Indian reservations seemed to be the only lands left suitable for Euro-American homesteading. Fifty thousand men had stampeded into Oklahoma Territory to mark claims on the first day the Territory was opened, April 22, 1889. Thousands more wanted the privilege of obtaining land at token prices. South Dakota became a state in November 1889, but most of its territory was the Great Sioux Reservation. Reservation Indians did not vote (the federal government extended citizenship to Indians in 1924, but some states denied them the vote as late as 1948). United States citizens—that is, Euro-Americans—in South Dakota, and those still living in

Figure 5. Lakota Sioux community at Cherry Creek on the Cheyenne River Sioux Reservation, South Dakota, in the 1880s.

the East who wanted to homestead, did vote. The elected representatives of the citizens of the United States set up a commission in March 1889 to work out an agreement with the Sioux to allot family farmsteads to Indian men and take the land remaining after allotment out of reservation status, opening it for non-Indian homesteading.

On February 10, 1890, five reservations were established on portions of what had been the Great Sioux Reservation of South Dakota. These five reservations constituted roughly half of the original Great Sioux Reservation. The other half was for sale to non-Indians at bargain prices, the proceeds to be paid to the Indians as compensation for their lost territory. Railroads received permission to survey and build lines, with little regard to Sioux concerns. On the five reservations, families were told to live on the 320-acre individual allotments instead of residing in multifamily camps or villages. They were to support themselves by agriculture, as instructed by Euro-American farmers hired as teachers by the Bureau of Indian Affairs: Their model was to be the self-sufficient European peasant family raising a variety of vegetables, fruit, grain, and livestock. Children were to be sent to boarding schools where they would be cut off from their Indian heritage and made to live Euro-American style, speaking English and subject to punishment if they talked even with each other in their native language.

To the Sioux, the actions of President Harrison's government were treachery. In 1868, Sioux leaders had agreed to the Fort Laramie Treaty, forfeiting

Figure 6. Lakota Sioux women painting a hide under a tipi-cover shade, Rosebud Sioux Reservation, South Dakota, late 1890s.

most of their hunting lands in exchange for the right in perpetuity to the Great Sioux Reservation, any change to be valid only if approved by a three-fourths majority vote of adult Indian men. The discovery of gold in the Black Hills portion of the Great Sioux Reservation had led to unauthorized invasion by Euro-Americans, which the United States government rectified not by sending the Army against the illegal settlers, but by declaring the Sioux must relinquish that part of their reservation west of the 103d meridian, the land of the Black Hills. No vote of Indian men, as the Fort Laramie Treaty provided for, was taken. The Sioux thus lost, in 1876, their best hunting lands. The drastic cuts in the Sioux lands in 1890 were, to the Sioux, a further instance of American duplicity.

Then rations were cut. The United States had been providing food to Indian families on the reservations, partly as compensation for ceded lands and partly to support the families until they could develop their own farms to the point of self-sufficiency. Because the Great Sioux Reservation lay in the semi-arid zone of the Plains, European-style mixed farming could not succeed there. Most of the land was suited only to range. Indians worked hard in the spring of 1890 to plant crops as directed by their farm instructors, but by summer, heat and lack of rain had killed a substantial portion of the expected yield. Hunting was no longer an alternative resource, with the Black Hills lost and the bison herds of the Plains exterminated a few years earlier, in the early 1880s. Rations were needed as never before. Officials in Washington responded by blaming the Sioux for laziness and obstinacy in taking up the "civilized" ways of European farmers. The government *cut* rations to less than half of what had been issued only four years before. Sioux families faced starvation.

Sioux leaders protested the injustice of Congress' unilaterally taking half the lands reserved by treaty, and the cruelty of cutting rations. Those leaders who persisted in calling attention to the wrongs dealt their people were labeled troublemakers and threatened with imprisonment. The situation was so shameful that a group of East Coast citizens, organized as the National Indian Defense Association, encouraged an advocate, Caroline Weldon, to travel west to assist the Indians. Weldon, a widow, took her only child with her. The boy died from an infection, but the bereft woman persevered, gaining the friendship of the famous Hunkpapa Sioux leader Sitting Bull and pressing local officials to recognize the rights of the Sioux. She abandoned her mission only when she realized the Indians were more astute than she in gauging the hopelessness of battling a coalition of voting homesteaders, railroad builders, other businesses, and churches who received government funds for running Indian schools.

Throughout 1890, thousands of Indians danced the Paiute round dance proselytized through Jack Wilson's gospel. Many felt uplifted by the release of tension through hours of circling rhythmically, and strengthened by the fellowship of the celebrants. Others were excited by the prophecies told by

Figure 7. Cattle to be issued as rations to the Sioux, Rosebud Reservation, about 1889.

Figure 8. Lakota Sioux butchering cattle issued as beef ration, Rosebud Sioux Reservation, early 1890s.

those who fell into a trance. Some simply figured that if it were true that the earth would be renewed by enough Indians dancing, it was worth trying, and if their efforts did not succeed, nothing had been lost. Without bison to hunt, with the crops they had planted mostly destroyed by drought, Plains Indians in 1890 had plenty of time on their hands. President Harrison's new Commissioner of Indian Affairs, Thomas J. Morgan, discouraged the practice of traditional religious rituals and secular amusements as well. He ordered, in July 1890, that the recent custom of pretending to hunt the beef rations—cattle shipped to the reservations for slaughter would be let out of the corral and killed as if they were running bison—should be abolished, the cattle to be slaughtered "humanely" out of sight of the community. Morgan particularly forbade the participation of numbers of people in butchering the cattle: He considered the practice of whole communities working together at the carcasses, helping themselves to tasty morsels as they labored, a disgusting "savage" holdover from a banned way of life. With so many community activities denied and the pressure on Indian families to disband their villages and move onto separate farms, the impetus to join together for a few days of prayerful celebration was strong.

Sitting Bull, the famous Indian friend of Buffalo Bill Cody, was living in a village on Standing Rock Reservation in northern South Dakota in 1890. Numbers of villagers were dancing the Ghost Dance. Agent James McLaughlin of Standing Rock angrily told Sitting Bull that the "messiah doctrine" was "absurd" and that Sitting Bull should stop his people from dancing. Sitting Bull replied, most reasonably, that he and McLaughlin should journey together to Nevada and check out the "messiah" firsthand. If upon direct inspection the man's preaching should appear to be a false gospel, Sitting Bull promised McLaughlin that he would not hesitate to enlighten his people and urge them to give up the ritual. McLaughlin refused the challenge, charging that Sitting Bull was uncooperative, and he threatened the dignified leader with jail. Hunkpapa continued to dance in Sitting Bull's village. On November 19, 1890, McLaughlin asked his superiors for permission to withhold all rations from Indians who remained in Sitting Bull's village: Only Indians who moved to the agency where they could be strictly supervised would be issued food. Winter set in late in 1890—heavy snows had not yet buried the reservation— but by late November edible plants were gone, animals were in their winter refuges, and living off the open prairies would not be feasible. Could the people disregard McLaughlin?

Meanwhile, at Pine Ridge Reservation in southern South Dakota, a newly appointed agent named Royer dashed off, on October 30, a frightened letter to the Bureau of Indian Affairs:

> Your Department has been informed of the damage resulting from these dances [Ghost Dance] and of the danger attending them of the crazy Indians doing serious damage to others and the different Agencies I suppose report about the same but I have carefully studied the matter for nearly six weeks [actually, Royer had been at Pine Ridge only three weeks] and have brought all the persuasion to bear on the leaders that was possible but without effect and the only remedy for this matter is the use of military and until this is done you need not expect any progress from these people on the other hand you will be made to realize that they are tearing down more in a day than the Government can build in a month. (quoted in Utley 1963:105)

Two weeks later, after telegrams from Royer complaining that his Indian police had been defied by a man wanted for killing cattle, President Harrison ordered the Secretary of War to suppress "any threatened outbreak" (quoted by Utley 1963:111).

On November 20, 1890, troops of the United States Army marched into Pine Ridge and neighboring Rosebud Reservation agencies. An armed guard was stationed at the Oglala boarding school, making the hundred Sioux children in it hostages. Euro-American settlers, missionaries, and many Sioux afraid of being caught in hostilities came to the agencies to camp under military protection. At least twenty-one newspaper correspondents rushed to Pine Ridge, including Teresa Howard Dean of the *Chicago Herald*, perhaps the first woman war correspondent. The popular western painter Frederic Remington came out to sketch events for *Harper's Weekly*, and the *Illustrated American* sent the anthropologist Warren K. Moorehead. When nothing happened, the reporters assiduously collected and relayed back rumors. General Nelson Miles, said to be eyeing a nomination to the Presidency, told the Washington press corps that "it is a more comprehensive plot than anything ever inspired by Tecumseh, or even Pontiac" (quoted in Utley 1963:127).

Less belligerent officials in both Washington and the West urged placating the Sioux by restoring their quota of rations. The Secretary of the Interior ordered, on December 1, that enough rations be issued to fulfill the monthly amount set in the treaty. With a cold winter upon them and the messiah's resurrection of the earth not expected until spring, numbers of Indian bands came into the agencies. The people felt humiliated, and the young men resented their elders' seeking peace at all costs—after all, the older men had won glory in wars such as the Battle of the Little Bighorn, but youths reaching manhood had no avenue open to gain renown. The needs of their families forced the Indians to accept the rations.

Thousands of Army troops were now deployed in the vicinities of the Sioux reservations. Agent McLaughlin at Standing Rock was still convinced that Sitting Bull, harboring Ghost Dancing at his little settlement, was a dangerous enemy. McLaughlin would not give up his ambition, cherished for months, of packing his Hunkpapa opponent off to a federal prison. He commanded the agency's Indian policemen to arrest Sitting Bull—to bring him in at any cost. The police rushed his cabin at dawn on December 15, 1890. The old man was sleeping. The police allowed him to dress and stood with him outside the door of his cabin while his favorite horse, given to him by his friend and sometime employer Cody, was saddled. Sitting Bull's people gathered about, angry at the arrest. One man pulled out his rifle and shot one of the policemen. Falling, the policeman shot Sitting Bull. Another policeman, holding a gun to the old man's head, shot him, too. Police and men of the village battled, with killings on both sides, as Sitting Bull's two wives wailed their lament.

Later, there were accusations that McLaughlin hated Sitting Bull, who was in effect his rival for control of the Hunkpapa, and that McLaughlin's orders to his Indian policemen contained a coded command to kill Sitting Bull. McLaughlin of course denied this. It does seem that it was one of Sitting Bull's followers who fired first. On the other hand, had McLaughlin been more reasonable and conceded Sitting Bull's right to live as he wished, peace-

Figure 9. Indian police force. Rosebud Sioux agency, South Dakota, 1888.

Figure 10. Men of Big Foot's band of Miniconjou Lakota Sioux, dressed for a Grass Dance (now known as the men's traditional powwow dance), August 1890. Left to right, Bear That Runs and Crawls, Warrior, One Tooth Gone, Solo, and Make It Long [Sioux names usually refer to noteworthy personal or family events; the translations are often inadequate]. Most of these men were killed the following December at Wounded Knee.

ably, in his own village, no Indian policemen would have been holding cocked pistols to Sitting Bull's head at daybreak on December 15. In the end, Sitting Bull's horse expressed the real outcome of the affair: The animal had been trained by Buffalo Bill to "dance" when a gun was fired in the Wild West Show, and when it heard the gunfire as it was led to its master's cabin, it began to dance. The Indians said that Sitting Bull had been martyred for refusing to give up his religion, but the faith would not die. The horse was now dancing the Ghost Dance. The white man could not kill the messiah's flame.

Another Sioux chief would be martyred this miserable December. He was Big Foot, leader of a band of Miniconjou (properly, Mnikowoju) who, like the Hunkpapa, are a division of the Teton (Lakota) or western Sioux. Big Foot was noted for his skill as a diplomat, and for years had been called upon to negotiate disagreements. Because he was a band leader, he was on the Army list of potential troublemakers, his reputation as a peacemaker not-withstanding. When the troops moved in around the reservations, the commander at Fort Bennett was told to arrest Big Foot. The commander knew Big Foot and the situation at his village, and knew that the chief, far from raising trouble, was the principal means of quelling it. Therefore, he delayed executing the order for the chief's arrest. Then Big Foot was invited to come to the Pine Ridge agency to help negotiate a settlement of the Sioux grievances

Figure 11. Lakota Sioux camped at Pine Ridge agency, South Dakota.

over inadequate rations and their right to practice religious rituals. Fort Bennett's commander wanted Big Foot to come in to that fort, to prove that he was not hostile and would obey orders. Big Foot considered the call to join his fellow chiefs at Pine Ridge more important, and, with his entire village, he started on the trail south to Pine Ridge.

A group of diehard Ghost Dancers led by the evangelist Kicking Bull and his brother-in-law Short Bull were at this time camped on a fortress-like butte north of the Pine Ridge agency, between it and Big Foot's village. General Nelson Miles, out to win this new Indian war, interpreted Big Foot's traveling south to indicate that the old chief meant to disobey orders and add his men to the "hostiles" camped on the butte. A detachment of troops went out to intercept Big Foot. The chief explained to the major in charge that he, with all the families in his band, was endeavoring to join the negotiating leaders at Pine Ridge. The major saw that Big Foot was seriously ill, lying in his wagon bundled in blankets (he had caught pneumonia), but the major determined to escort the band to a camping place outside the now crowded Pine Ridge agency. Big Foot and his people were to set up their tipis that night beside Wounded Knee Creek.

The band pitched their tipis that December 28 in the creek valley. Around them were the tents of the cavalry troops and of Indian scouts attached to the Army. On the valley wall overlooking the camp were stationed two Hotchkiss artillery cannons. In the Indian camp were 120 men and 230 women and children. First thing in the morning on December 29, 1890, the Sioux were commanded to turn in all their weapons. A pile of guns was soon collected, but the Army officers in charge of the disarmament noticed they were mostly old muskets, not the good rifles many of the Indian men had been seen carrying the day before. The officers searched the tipis, politely lifting up women sitting on their bedding and sometimes discovering guns hidden under them. Still

Figure 12. Big Foot's frozen body after the battle, Wounded Knee, 1890.

there seemed too few good weapons collected. The officers turned to the men of the band, herded into a group by the soldiers. Yellow Bird, the band's native doctor and spirutual leader (in Lakota, *wicaša wakan*, "holy man"), had been Ghost Dancing all by himself around the group of men. An interpreter heard him reminding the men that the shirts they wore for their new faith protected them from bullets. The Army officers ordered the Indian men to open the blankets they wore pulled about them on the cold December morning. Slowly, the older men obeyed. No weapons were revealed, and the men were told to stand aside. The younger men stood impassive, refusing to comply with the order. The officers began to frisk them one by one. Suddenly a deaf and generally despised young man, Black Coyote, stepped out, waving a rifle above his head, yelling that he had paid good money for the gun and wouldn't give it for nothing. Two soldiers rushed over to him, grabbing his rifle from behind. Yellow Bird threw a handful of dirt—symbolic of the renewal of the earth promised by the messiah—into the air as Black Coyote's rifle discharged in his struggle with the two soldiers. His bullet went harmlessly into the air, but several other young Sioux men threw off their blankets and leveled their concealed rifles at the rank of soldiers.

Sioux volley met Army carbines. Bullets that missed men hit the tipis in which the women and children waited. Big Foot, lying in a tent the Army had given him, raised himself in bed and was killed. Sioux and soldiers wrestled in hand-to-hand combat with knives and pistols as the Indian men fought to get away from the camp, to draw the enemy into the open where opposing

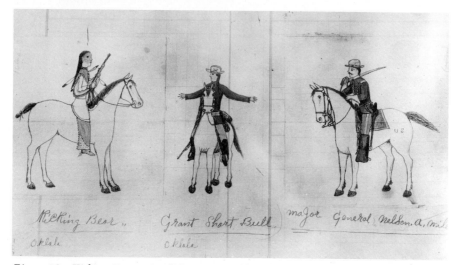

Kicking Bear

Oklala

Grant Short Bull

Oklala

major General nelson a. mil

Figure 13. Kicking Bear surrendering to General Nelson Miles, 1891. (Grant Short Bull carried messages between the opponents.) Drawn by Amos Bad Heart Bull, an Oglala Lakota Sioux artist.

sides could be drawn up and where the Indians could retreat up a ravine as they shot at the soldiers. As the men broke from the camp, the artillery cannons trained on it fired round after round. Women and their children dashed from the tipis, running toward the same ravine their men had raced into. Yellow Bird dashed into a tent belonging to the Indian scouts and from it shot soldier after soldier until one of the artillery guns lobbed two shells into it; enraged soldiers then threw bales of hay against the tent and lit them, cremating Yellow Bird's body inside.

After protracted fighting along the ravine, the Miniconjous seemed to have been conquered when a reinforcement of Oglalas and Brulés, the Sioux camped around Pine Ridge agency, rode over the ridge. The contingent from Pine Ridge exchanged fire with the soldiers, then rode off taking with them the Miniconjous able to escape. The Army counted 39 dead on their side, 153 on the Sioux. In addition, an unknown number of Indians died away from the battlefield, among their own people or lost on the prairie in the blizzard sweeping in. Of the 146 Sioux collected for mass burial at the Wounded Knee camp, 44 were women and 18, little children.

Sioux at Pine Ridge agency fled at the news of the massacre, forming armed parties between their families and the troops they feared meant to add to the carnage. As it became evident that the Wounded Knee disaster had not been a planned slaughter—that it was a tragedy sparked by panic on both sides—the Sioux returned, band by band, to surrender to the Army commanders. Last of all, on January 15, 1891, came Kicking Bear the evangelist, who for the second time—he had previously surrendered to him in 1877—gave up his rifle to General Miles.

Figure 14. Kicking Bear speaking at the meeting of Lakota Sioux leaders, Pine Ridge agency, South Dakota, January 1891.

Figure 15. Two Strike, Crow Dog, and High Hawk, three leaders of the Lakota Sioux, surrendering at Pine Ridge agency, January 1891.

Buffalo Bill Cody's dancing horse had marked the death of Sitting Bull. Now Cody invited Kicking Bear, Short Bull, and the twenty-three other Sioux leaders held prisoner by General Miles to join his Wild West Show on its upcoming European tour. Miles protested that the men belonged in the penitentiary, but the Secretary of the Interior intervened on behalf of the popular hero of the West, and the Sioux prisoners were released to Buffalo Bill, to be highlights of his new show. Back home, the Sioux people settled again into their reservation villages. Congress, shocked by news accounts of the desperation of hungry Sioux that had driven them, it was said, to a final stand at Wounded Knee, legislated increased appropriations for the reservations. Included in the sums was money to compensate the Indians for confiscated goods. It was too late for Black Coyote.

Figure 16. The mass grave of the Lakota Sioux killed at Wounded Knee, December 29, 1890. Photographed by anthropologist James Mooney in 1891.

3/Death or Renewal?

Popular wisdom has it that the Ghost Dance was the death throes of a vanishing race. From the days of the Puritan colonizers of the middle 1600s, English invaders of what became the United States wanted to believe that the native peoples of America should not stand in the way of Europeans. The Puritans interpreted an epidemic that had decimated Massachusetts Indian villages to be a sign that God would clear the land for the Puritans' New Jerusalem. When Britain embarked upon an aggressive expansion of its mercantile economy at the end of the seventeenth century, the philosopher-politician John Locke, serving on Britain's Board of Trade, wrote that it would be a "just [that is, justifiable] war" if Britain conquered peoples such as the American Indians who did not divide the lands into private properties in a money-based market economy. After the American Revolution, Thomas Jefferson prepared a basic policy for United States relationships with the Indians, outlining a process of drawing Indians into debt for goods from government-operated trading posts, then pressuring the Indians to discharge their debts by ceding land. In theory, the Indians would by then have given up hunting for agriculture and would need less land than formerly. He argued that no injustice would be done because, as he wrote with his usual eloquence, "In leading them thus to agriculture, to manufactures, and civilization, . . . in preparing them ultimately to participate in the benefits of our Government, I trust and believe we are acting for their greatest good" (quoted in Prucha 1984:139).

Europeans and their descendants in America seldom doubted they had a divine mission to "civilize" the Indians. Only radicals and rascals entertained the possibility that there were alternative and equally good ways of living. Christians read in their Bibles that they were to go out throughout the world converting people to a Christian life, and for the vast majority of Christians, a "Christian life" was one lived according to European customs and laws. American Indians who, offered the opportunity, refused to engage in European societies' occupations, live in European-style houses, dress in contemporary European fashion, and use the English language were savages damning themselves to eternal misery. Most United States officials and other citizens honestly believed this, although it is true that the belief can be cynically viewed as the "cant of conquest," as historian Francis Jennings labels it: The conviction served to legitimatize, in Euro-American minds, United

States power exercised against those who happened to be in the way of United States economic and political interests.

Throughout the nineteenth century, American Indian groups moved west with the frontier of United States settlement. Jefferson had suggested, when he arranged the Louisiana Purchase, that Indians east of the Mississippi might thereby be induced to migrate beyond the frontier into territories newly under United States jurisdiction. The War of 1812 interrupted the implementation of such ideas, but they came into favor again after its conclusion. Ironically, pressure to emigrate was applied to those Indians who best exemplified Jefferson's ideal of assimilation to European culture, especially the Cherokee in Georgia. Cherokees had always lived by farming, and after British colonies were built near them, they adopted many methods and crops from their European neighbors. By the 1820s, Cherokee were reading their own newspaper published in both English and Cherokee, most dressed as Europeans, and some owned fine plantations worked by black slaves. Their very success brought them into constant conflict with Georgia citizens coveting these farmlands. The case of the Cherokee proved that Jefferson's dream could not be achieved, for, in the final analysis, the issue was ownership of resources. No matter how "civilized" an Indian people might become, so long as they controlled resources craved by Euro-Americans, they were seen as opposed to "progress." Only by getting out of the way of "Americans" could Indians live in peace.

Until the Civil War in the 1860s, removal west of the Mississippi was the panacea for Indian troubles. The Cherokee and dozens of other Indian nations in eastern North America trekked beyond the frontier to Indian Territory, in what is now Oklahoma, and adjacent states. The emigrants of course took space among the Indian nations already in the West, causing waves of battles over territory. Euro-Americans continuously pushed west, too, until, at the time of the Civil War, the Midwest was fully occupied and those seeking bargain farmland looked to the Plains beyond the Mississippi Valley. There, the semi-arid climate restricted farming to river valley bottoms; most of the country was open grassland supporting herds of bison, the principal food of the Plains Indians. Euro-American homesteaders tried raising wheat and cattle, while other immigrants opened businesses supplying the new towns, the wagon trains of travelers, and the crews building railroads. Between increased predation by the larger numbers of Indians forced to live by hunting in the West, the curtailment of bison grazing brought about by Euro-American settlement, and the wholesale slaughter of herds for the hide market, the bison were depleted to the point of extinction by the early 1880s. The Indians' staff of life was broken.

From the end of the Civil War in 1865 to the 1880s, the United States waged war on the Indians, determined to crush any hindrance to the American vision of a nation dominant "from sea to shining sea." British Canada and Mexico were no longer threats. The United States Army had no other enemies to engage it but the Indians recalcitrant to give up their homelands. The full force of the professional Army, supported by a nation building itself into one of the world's major industrial powers, was turned to win the West. Several factors undermined Indian resistance: Indian populations were again and again cut by epidemics, which hit the small Indian communities unusually hard by often killing the able-bodied adults upon whom the bands depended; Indian populations received few recruits from outside, while the United States was vastly enlarging its population with millions of immigrants from Europe; the bison, the only dependable resource for Indians on the Plains, were disappearing, overhunted and driven from their grazing ranges; and the repeated betrayals of treaty agreements by United States agents caused crises of leadership among the Indians. There was no lack of intelligent, dedicated men and women among the Indians fighting for their homes, as General Custer discovered in his defeat at the Little Bighorn, but the Indians could not sustain their war with their losses of people and of their subsistence resource.

The United States termed its war against the western Indians a policy of pacification. (Since St. Augustine's time, European culture has harbored the cockeyed logic that to make peace, you have to be waging war.) Once an Indian nation surrendered its arms, it would be confined to a reservation and pressured into practicing Euro-American customs, including Christianity. This was "civilizing" the "savage." Being "savage," the Indian peoples had to be ignorant of what was good, and need not be consulted about their wishes. There was no lack of Euro-Americans, in eastern cities and in reservation agency towns, who knew what the Indian needed and were prepared to sacrifice money, effort, and even comfortable careers in the East to enable Indians to "progress" toward "civilization." The wars of pacification were said to be unfortunately necessary steps toward this goal. Most American citizens supported these wars without compunction.

Once it became apparent, around 1880, that Indian resistance was effectively broken, associations of Christian citizens were formed in the East to push for civilian domination in relations with the Indians. Churches expanded their missions, contracting with the government to run schools for Indians. This arrangement looks unconstitutional to us today, but nineteenth-century Americans tended to ignore the Founding Fathers' separation of state from church. The Commissioner of Indian Affairs from 1889 to 1893 under President Benjamin Harrison, Thomas Jefferson Morgan, was a Baptist minister who had served as head of school systems in three states. Not surprisingly, Morgan favored education in church-affiliated schools as the means to achieve his namesake's vision of assimilating Indians into national American society "for their greatest good."

The massacre at Wounded Knee on December 29, 1890 raised a storm among citizens in the East because it seemed so cruelly unnecessary. The public had been told the pacification of the Indians was virtually complete. The Sioux nation was down, and decent people don't kick a man when he's down. Shooting fleeing women with babies is an atrocity. The Sioux had been treated shamefully. Easterners distrusted South Dakotans' story that the Ghost Dance was a sinister gathering to foment rebellion. They found it easier to believe that the poor unhappy savages, bereft of their untutored pleasures in the hunt and disillusioned with the failures of their tribal fetishes to protect them, had turned in foolish hope to the rumor of a messiah sent to them. Reform associations attacked the politics that had recalled an experienced agent from Pine Ridge and replaced him with the party flunky Royer. The easy subjugation of the Sioux in January 1891, great as were their grievances, proved the incapacity of the savages to seriously threaten the United States. Their "Ghost Dance" must have been a childlike fantasy.

At the Smithsonian Institution, the anthropologist James Mooney was skeptical of both views of the Ghost Dance—that it was sinister or that it was foolish. His years of friendships with a variety of Indians, from Cherokees holed up in remote hollows of the Great Smokies to Kiowas out on the western Plains, had impressed him that Indians were truly his fellow humans. His own background, son of dirt-poor and despised Irish immigrants, gave him a strong feeling of fellowship with other groups conquered and oppressed by English-speaking governments. Mooney persuaded his superiors to assign him to investigate the "messiah rumor" and the tragedy of Wounded Knee. From this he would write a classic study, *The Ghost-Dance Religion and Wounded Knee*, published by the Smithsonian in 1896 (and reprinted in an inexpensive paperback by Dover in 1973). He would conclude that Jack Wilson was a true prophet founding a real religion, and he would favorably compare Wilson and his religion to others in Western history, including Christianity.

To know the Ghost Dance religion, one must start out, as James Mooney realized, in Mason Valley, Nevada. Jack Wilson was born and died a Tövusi-dökadö, member of a loose community of Paiutes in Mason Valley. The region, western Nevada, was occupied for many centuries by people we call Northern Paiutes. Their language, Paiute, is related to that of the Utes and Shoshoni and Comanche, and to that of Hopi Pueblo, the Pima and Papago in Arizona, and, through a series of northwestern Mexican Indian nations, the Aztecs whose empire had its magnificent capital in what is now Mexico City. In favorable environments, it is clear, societies of this Uto-Aztecan language stock developed complex civilizations that rivaled any in medieval Europe. In a desert environment such as Nevada, Uto-Aztecans adapted to sparse resources.

Northern Paiute formed communities based on harvesting the foods in a valley and its surrounding hills. Each group was known by the name of its principal local resource. Mason Valley people were the Tövusi-dökadö, "Cyperus-bulb Eaters." (Cyperus is a marsh plant, related to Egyptian papyrus, with seeds encased in a bulb-like covering.) Mason Valley, in west-ernmost Nevada southwest of Walker Lake, joins feeder streams from the Sierra Nevada to form Walker River leading to Walker Lake. Paiute families who got along well together cooperated to construct and use fish dams and fishing platforms in season, to harvest pine nuts in the mountains in the fall, and occasionally to drive antelope, rabbits, or mud hens through large sections of the valley into nets or under the clubs of people positioned to intercept the animals.

Tövusi-dökadö were simply those Paiute living and cooperating in Mason

Valley. They had no permanent officials. Organized activities, such as antelope drives, or religious celebrations, such as of harvests, were directed by people who believed themselves to have been granted spiritual power to lead the activity. For example, a "rabbit boss" would have had a dream or similar vision in which he felt a spirit promised him success in rabbit drives. Such a leader prayed at the beginning of the operation to activate the spirit power and thanked the spirit in prayer at the conclusion of the activity. Realistically, Paiute who were vouchsafed spiritual power apprenticed themselves to experienced practitioners before venturing to lead an activity on their own. Most organized activities, whether for harvesting food or for ceremonies, were expected to last five days.

"Doctors" were spiritually blessed, like "bosses," to carry out particular activities. Doctors gifted to heal the sick had bouts of illness before realizing that they were being called by a spirit to master the disease. These doctors safeguarded their hard-won mastery over an illness by obeying the spirit's warning to follow certain practices or precautions, such as bathing at dawn or avoiding salt, and prayed and made small offerings to express their gratitude for the spirit's aid. They exercised this aid by sucking at the place in a patient's body where the pain seemed to reside, drawing the illness out, they believed. Paiutes used also a variety of medicinal plants.

Figure 17. Ocheo in front of his wickiup—a typical Paiute scene, late nineteenth century.

"Weather doctors" mastered the weather through spiritual aid, as healing doctors mastered illnesses. Tavibo, Jack Wilson's father, was known as an adept at controlling weather, and his son followed in his footsteps, a frequent occurrence in the families of doctors. As with other kinds of power, the weather doctor perfected the exercise of the spiritual gift by watching and assisting a successful practicing doctor. Paiutes said weather doctors controlled storms and winds and could make drought, rain, or snow.

People came to the appropriate doctor or boss for assistance in crises, whether personal illness or misfortune or widespread need for obtaining subsistence. To thank the spirits who empowered the doctor or boss, Paiutes gave gifts to the adept. Paiute society appeared egalitarian, but underneath the informality, the sharing of resources, and individuals' right to join or leave a group as they pleased, Paiutes recognized differences in ability. Certain families, like Tavibo's, trained their children to seek greater responsibility, to expect to be selected by spirits to assist ordinary folk. Communities looked for evidence of special gifts in these families. Tavibo and his son Wovoka (Jack Wilson) earned their leadership by study and responsible practice, though all believed their ultimate source of power was the blessing by spirits.

Wovoka (the name means "Cutter") was born about 1860, probably in Mason Valley. The year he was born, a U.S. Army post, Fort Churchill, was built a few miles north of Mason Valley to "pacify" Paiutes who might object to colonists taking over their land. Throughout Wovoka's boyhood, Euro-Americans came into Mason and the adjoining valleys and developed cattle ranches along the rich valley bottoms where the Tövusi-dökadö had harvested seeds. Mason Valley colonists were men with families planning to earn a steady income through selling beef rather than gambling on striking it rich in the mines elsewhere in Nevada. These ranchers needed laborers and hired Tövusi-dökadö who accepted wage work as one more resource in their valley. Of course, any Paiute who publicly objected to wage work replacing harvesting tövusi seeds could see Fort Churchill as a reminder that he or she did not have much choice.

Ranchers like David Wilson, who came to Mason Valley in 1863, learned to speak Paiute. They let their children play with the Paiute children while Paiute women washed clothes and did household chores for ranch families. Paiute men worked as cowboys, dug and maintained irrigation ditches, cut wood for winter fuel, and, with the women, cut and stacked hay in season. The work could be hard, but the Indians did not see it as tedious, and the Paiute families took breaks to fish, hunt, and collect pine nuts. Indians were paid nearly as much as "whites" for their labor, and they felt themselves comfortably off.

In 1867, several hundred Paiutes from Fish Lake Valley and adjacent localities on the California-Nevada border, south of Walker River, migrated to fish in Walker Lake. Their leader was called Fish Lake Joe, and known also as *wodziwob*, "white hair," meaning that he was a person who had received a call to become a doctor in adulthood rather than, as more usual, in childhood. Fish Lake Joe married a Walker River Paiute woman and settled near a place named Hawthorne, whence he got the name Hawthorne Wod-ziwob. He lived until about 1920, and was famous for being able to bring back souls that had just left sick bodies. To accomplish this spirit-endowed power, he would lie next to the patient and go into a trance, sending his own soul after the patient's to fetch it back, thereby reviving the body.

In 1867, an epidemic of typhoid and other diseases killed one-tenth of the Walker River Paiutes. The next spring, in 1868, twenty-five Paiutes, mostly children, died of measles. Such a large number of deaths not only caused great grief, but disrupted the Paiute economy. Many families had not been able to move about as usual to follow game and harvest pine nuts. Instead, they ended up in the rough mining town of Virginia City looking for wage work. Wodziwob had a dream empowering him, he believed, to lead the souls of those who died in the previous months back to their mourning families. This was an extension of his regular power, which worked only close to the moment of apparent death. In 1869, Wodziwob organized a series of community dances, possibly the regular pine nut harvest festival, and announced his extended power. Since Wodziwob had successfully restored dying individuals to life, the Paiutes were receptive to his new claim. He exhorted them to ornament themselves with paint as they usually did for festivals and to dance the common round dance. When the people stopped to rest, Wodziwob fell into a trance. Awakening, he reported that his soul had journeyed over the mountains to the land of the dead, had seen the dead happy in this land, and had extracted promises from the souls to return to their loved ones, perhaps in three or four years. The survivors along Walker River were to be pleased with this news. A local weather doctor, Tavibo, admired this *wodziwob* and helped spread his prophecy.

A drought began in 1869, drying up pine nuts and grass seeds, and forcing the Paiutes during the next two years to rely much more on fish, which strained the fish populations of Walker River and Lake. Ranchers during these years were cutting irrigation ditches in the valley, disrupting the flow of the river and leading many fish to die in these dead-end artificial channels. By 1872, fish were scarce, plant foods were not to be had, and Paiute were starving. For four years, they had been dancing, hopefully, at Wodziwob's direction. Now he had another dream: Now he saw that what he had supposed were happy souls were only shadows. An owl, denizen of darkness, mocked him as he gazed at the empty shadows. Wodziwob realized with horror that his prophecy was no more than a cruel trick of the evil witch owl. He confessed his sad disillusion to the Paiutes, and they ceased dancing to attract back their loved ones.

The idea of a return of the dead had meanwhile spread to much-bereaved Indians far beyond Nevada, in Oregon and California. Its glimmer of hope inspired prophets and priests in other Indian nations to reorganize their peoples' worship, often left chaotic by the recent deaths in epidemics and wars of so many spiritual leaders. California Indians were especially hard hit because, it addition to epidemics, armed conflicts, and malnutrition suffered when they were driven out of their homelands, they had been the target of

Sunday afternoon sport by the lawless Gold Rush prospectors, who amused themselves shooting anything that moved—deer, rabbits, Indians. Wodziwob's dance was the means of regrouping communities. If it failed to revive dead persons, it did revive the surviving Indians' determination to forge ways of life compatible with their present circumstances. They worked out new ceremonies, amalgamations of old, borrowed, and newly invented rituals, and made these the center of community life. Much of the "1870 Ghost Dance" religious revival among California Indians was institutionalized into beliefs and practices that continue today.

In Mason Valley, the drought broke in 1873, and Paiutes who had planted small farms reaped their own crops for the first time. Wovoka was a boy at this time, the oldest of three surviving sons of the weather doctor Tavibo, who had assisted the *wodziwob* Fish Lake Joe. Tavibo, who lived until about 1910, traveled extensively. He very likely trained his eldest child to follow in his practice, as Paiute doctors usually did, but all that is recorded about Wovoka's youth is that he was given work on the David Wilson ranch and, with the job, the English name Jack Wilson. (This was standard in that period: Each Tövusi-dökadö family ended up with the surname of the Euro-American colonist who regularly employed that family.) Before long, even the other Paiutes began to call Wovoka by his American name.

David Wilson liked young Jack. Bright and lively, the boy quickly became a pal of Wilson's two sons, working beside them on the ranch and attending with them the family evening prayers, grace at meals, and regular Bible reading. Mason Valley began to seem small to Jack in about 1880, when he was around twenty, and he left, together with hundreds of other Indians, to work in the hop harvests in Oregon, Washington, and northern California. (Hops are a fruit used to flavor beer.) Owners of hop fields recruited Indian labor from all over the Northwest, so people from a great diversity of Indian tribes camped together, talked with one another about their customs and beliefs, and partied together when they were paid at season's end. Through these camps, Jack Wilson learned of prophets who had founded Indian churches.

Smohalla ("The Preacher") was one of the best-known prophets in the Northwest. He was a Wanapum from the northern Columbia River Valley, on the Washington-Idaho border. In about 1860, Smohalla, then approximately forty years old, lost a battle with a rival Indian people. He thought it wise to be absent until his friends recovered from the bitterness of defeat, and traveled down the Columbia River all the way to the Pacific, then south to Mexico, and finally home via Arizona and Utah. His people thought he had been killed in the battle—he had been so badly wounded that he himself may have thought he died but revived—and were ready to believe his claim that he had been to the country of the spirits and now returned with a vital message: Indians should cease to follow the white invaders' way, cease to plow and mine the earth; they should take only the resources freely given on the earth's surface and in the waters. So Indians had done before the invasions, and in those days they had not suffered such fighting, hunger, and disease as now beset them. Smohalla's message seemed reasonable, since it was true that a host of diseases and displacement from resources had come with the invading colonists. "The Preacher" held Sunday worship services incorporating ritual elements from Roman Catholicism, such as a boy bell-ringer accompanying the priest in procession, but Smohalla said the symbols referred to Indian beliefs. From time to time, he announced new messages received when his soul journeyed to the Creator as his body lay in a trance. He could control the weather and eclipses. (A U.S. Army major investigated these claims, witnessing the authenticity of Smohalla's trance and inspired preaching when he revived himself. The major noticed, however, that when it came to controlling eclipses, The Preacher was assisted by reading an almanac.) Smohalla's religion became a symbol of repudiation of an alien, Euro-American way of life.

Jack Wilson heard about Smohalla's creed, and he heard the outrages suffered by so many Indians harassed by colonists, driven sometimes at gunpoint from their homes onto reservations on marginal lands where they were ordered to farm though they lacked tools, seeds, and stock. Jack worked beside Indians who saw no alternative to labor in the hop fields. He appreciated, as he had not earlier, the mutual decency Paiutes and colonists had shown in Mason Valley. Smohalla was a true prophet, but he was powerless to turn back the foreigners raping the beautiful earth of the Northwest.

By 1888, Jack Wilson was settled back in Mason Valley. He had married a young Paiute woman called Mary and was the happy father of a son. He worked for the Wilsons, but lived with his family and other Tövusi-dökadö in traditional Paiute style. The mining boom in Nevada was declining, and there were fewer of the get-rich-quick unscrupulous men so prone to cause trouble. Mason Valley had never attracted many of this type; ranching was all it offered. A rail line had been built into the Valley in 1883, making it easier to ship out beef, so ranchers were extending the irrigation systems to raise more crops and cattle. Chinese laborers were coming in to do the heaviest work. The Tövusi-dökadö felt secure in their little camps of tule-reed wickiups along the borders of the ranches.

The year 1888 brought repeated earth tremors in western Nevada. On January 1, 1889, a solar eclipse seemed to cap these disturbing tremors. Though he was ill, Jack Wilson used his weather-doctor power to end the tremors and bring back the sun. It was then, he told James Mooney exactly three years later, that his soul flew to heaven and received God's bidding to preach a gospel of peace. Jack Wilson faithfully carried out his mission. Not only did he speak as a prophet to the Paiutes, but he dictated letters to the local storekeeper, Edward Dyer, to send to more distant Indians inviting them to come hear. Early in the spring of 1889, Shoshoni and Arapaho from just east of the Rockies came to heap with gifts the blanket on which Jack Wilson sat as he instructed them. Tövusi-dökadö were proud that Tavibo's son was fulfilling his destiny. They organized dances such as they enjoyed at the pine nut harvest festivals, in honor now of their distinguished prophet and his visitors. To convince the skeptical of the authenticity of his relationship with God, Jack Wilson demonstrated his weather power: He caused ice to fall from the sky in July, he transplanted a tree during a fierce rain without getting wet, he lighted his pipe by simply pointing it toward the sun, he made water appear in an empty container during a drought, he ended the drought of 1889 in October and caused heavy rains from then to the following April. (Unfortunately, by October it was too late to save the hay crop, and many cattle died during the wet winter.)

In August 1889, Jack Wilson's power was mentioned to the local newspaper editor, who remarked, "The great weather prophet is said to be a fine looking man, much resembling the late Henry Ward Beecher." This comment suggests the mundane source of Jack Wilson's power: a commanding physical presence, a practiced gift for oratory, conviction of the truth of what he preached, and, not least, confidence born of being the admired son of a highly respected father. (The newspaper editor would have remembered that Henry Ward Beecher, the Billy Graham of nineteenth-century America—handsome, charismatic, the country's most popular preacher—was the son of minister and seminary president Lyman Beecher.) Jack Wilson could go into a trance to receive new revelations right in front of his audience, confirming to them his claim that he could send his soul out of his body to obtain spiritual knowledge. Using a technique familiar to many Indians, that of inducing hypnosis by waving eagle feathers (symbolizing heavenly flight) before a believer's face, he sent many participants in his dances into a trance where they, too, gained revelations. The weather doctor's powers included magical control over the thundering shotgun. Tövusi-dökadö saw him, at rabbit drives, load his gun with dust (in place of powder) and sand for shot, then take aim and kill a jackrabbit. Once, he demonstrated that he was invulnerable to shot: He loaded his gun as he did at rabbit drives with dust and sand, handed it to his younger brother, and went to stand on a blanket some yards away. The brother pulled the trigger, the gun went off with a bang, and when the smoke cleared, everyone saw Jack still standing on the blanket, his shirt riddled with holes and shot at his feet, but miraculously uninjured.

Storekeeper Dyer's memoir of his famous customer, interviews with rancher Wilson's sons and their families, and anthropologist Michael Hittman's research in the late 1960s with Mason Valley Paiutes who remembered Jack Wilson round out the picture of the prophet recorded by James Mooney in 1892. Jack Wilson was a formidable weather doctor who seemed to control natural phenomena and, by extension, individuals' personal "climate," making people feel more sunny, as it were, lifting their depression. Paiutes came to him steadily to be cured of illness and malaise. No one was surprised when Jack Wilson was invited to appear at the San Francisco Midwinter Fair in 1894 (as it turned out, he was seen as a sort of sideshow exhibition). In 1926, Wilson was still well-known enough to pose with the cowboy actor Tim McCoy, who was also Governor of Wyoming, when McCoy was filming a western near Walker Lake Reservation. Jack Wilson died of nephritis, a kidney disease, in September 1932. It took an earthquake in December 1932 to convince many Paiutes that the prophet had gone to the other world for

Figure 18. Jack Wilson (Wovoka), still a well-known doctor and leader, in a twentieth-century photograph.

good, announcing his soul's arrival as he had prophesied, by shaking the earth.

Jack Wilson was a secular leader as well as a doctor. In 1912, he headed a delegation of thirty Mason Valley Paiutes requesting forty-acre farm allotments from the Indian agent at Walker River Reservation. Like any other respectable Paiute family man, Jack Wilson worked for wages and in traditional subsistence pursuits. His doctor powers enabled him to supplement his income by selling blessed red ocher paint, magpie feathers, and items of his own clothing believed by some of his followers to be imbued with his spirituality. His distinctive black sombrero was especially desired, and storekeeper Dyer remembered that when a letter came requesting one, Jack Wilson would pull off the hat he was wearing, instructing Dyer to mail it with a bill for twenty dollars (when twenty dollars was a week's good wages). Dyer kept a generous stock of black sombreros and would immediately sell Jack a new one for a few dollars, wishing he could turn as great a profit on the hats as the prophet did. Jack Wilson apparently did not read or write English and used Dyer as a secretary; thus, Dyer knew the doctor's mail-order practice and estimated that it brought in about thirty-five dollars a month. The *Lyon County Times* hit it right when its editor compared him to Henry Ward Beecher, who was pretty well paid, too.

Mason Valley Paiutes appreciated Jack Wilson's leadership in so many facets of life. They felt lucky that so great a doctor was a Tövusi-dökadö, and addressed him as "Father," as Catholics call their priests Father, to denote respect, obedience to his wise leadership, and gratitude for his paternal concern. They listened to his inspiring preaching and sang the prayers he taught them, because his counsel and his personal conduct justified their faith. That he earned a nice income accepting money for spiritually charged objects was to them proof of his worth—even distant strangers benefited from this man's extraordinary powers. The spirits to whom he owed his gifts expected to be honored by such public acknowledgment.

For the Paiutes, Jack Wilson was a custodian of their tradition, guiding them in accommodating to the exigencies of United States invasion and colonization. Jack Wilson was more than a human leader to Indian peoples far away from Nevada. For the Teton Sioux (Lakota) in 1890, the messiah in the West was hope out of the chaos into which they had fallen. Tövusi-dökadö in 1890 lived on their ancestral lands, though they had to share them; fished, hunted, and gathered plant foods as they had for centuries, though they now interpolated wage work in the seasonal round; politely kept out of the way of Indian agents; and had little interference. Lakota had seen the bison herds disappear as if by divine command in retribution for the evils on the earth. Bison had been more than food and tipi covers; they were the manifestation of the Almighty's gift of life to the Lakota, and that gift had been withdrawn. Lakota families had been shoved out of this territory and then out of that, ordered to settle down contrary to their habits. Their leaders were threatened with jail when they protested injustices. Rational, reasonable, peace-seeking behavior could fail tragically, as would be seen again in Big Foot's death. Government promises turned into half rations and seizure of half the Great Sioux Reservation. Maybe, maybe, that man in the West, that man whose own people seemed to have accommodated the invasion, could help the Lakota.

Black Elk, an Oglala Lakota spiritual leader, said that in 1890 "the white man had taken our world from us and we were like prisoners of war" (Neihardt in De Mallie 1984:265). Black Elk had energetically danced the Ghost Dance then, flanked on one side by the evangelist Kicking Bear and on the other by Good Thunder, one of the Oglala sent by tribal leaders to evaluate Jack Wilson. (Good Thunder was planning to marry Black Elk's widowed mother and was encouraging the young man to follow the calling of his late father, a *wicaša wakan*, "holy man.") Falling into a trance, young Black Elk saw in visions the happy land of the spirits where the bison had gone. Holy persons spoke to him, in his visions, and charged him to return to earth and lead his people in worship as a means to restore the blessed life they led before the Indian Wars. After the Oglalas' final surrender in 1891, Black Elk worked for years as a catechist with the Catholic Church's Sioux missions. Eventually, Black Elk decided his mission to his people would be best fulfilled by returning to the Oglala religion of his youth. The Ghost Dance religion was foreign to the Oglalas in 1890, one of several new religions offered to the people after "their world was taken from them" in the 1880s. Proselytized by Kicking Bear, Jack Wilson's creed was distorted among the Lakota, becoming a millenarian movement yearning for utopia instead of the Paiute prophet's sensible guide to a clean, honest life. Distorted, the Ghost Dance seemed to fail the Lakotas.

Other Plains Indians did benefit from Jack Wilson's Ghost Dance religion. The Pawnee in 1890 had been removed from their Nebraska farmlands to an Oklahoma reservation. Malnourishment and epidemics took a heavy toll of the people. Many learned doctors and priests died suddenly without having fully passed on their knowledge and rituals to apprentices. Some who survived felt they could no longer practice because bison meat, used as a communion sacrament in rituals, and other traditional items were no longer available. In 1891, a Pawnee man, Frank White, attended Ghost Dance ceremonies among Comanche and Wichita, and was inspired to become the religion's evangelist for his people. The promise that one could see deceased loved ones while in Ghost Dance–induced trances brought hundreds of grieving Pawnee to White. Then a truly marvelous thing happened: People saw not only their relatives, but the dead doctors and priests in the visions. These leaders instructed the visionaries in the performance of the rituals and healing arts, and advised them to carry out the practices as best they could under the reservation circumstances. Pawnee culture was not lost after all!

Joyously, the Pawnee danced. With solemn excitement they pooled their memories to recapture the ceremonies. With respectful eagerness they listened to men and women who had envisioned feasible ways of performing the rituals. Far from being discouraged when the hoped-for extinction of the Euro-American invaders did not transpire, the Pawnee in 1904 sent three delegates to Nevada to improve their people's understanding of Jack Wilson's creed through personal discussion with the prophet. Camping together to enact ceremonies and enjoy traditional Pawnee social activities became the principal business of the Pawnee during the early decades of this century, when most of the Pawnee gained their income through the distribution of lease payments from Euro-Americans for the use of tribal lands. Most of the Pawnee crafts, costumes, and ritual paraphernalia collected by anthropologists for museums are not pre-reservation objects but replicas inspired by the Ghost Dance visions after 1891.

Among his own people and among those such as the Pawnee who understood Jack Wilson's message of peaceable accommodation, the Ghost Dance

Figure 19. A performance of the Ghost Dance organized by James Mooney for the Trans-Mississippian and International Exposition, Omaha, Nebraska, September 1898.

religion strengthened Indian communities. Its ritual and creed were simple but no more "primitive" than the Sermon on the Mount. It failed to achieve institutional structure and persistence as Christianity did, but, except for the Lakota episode, it avoided the distortions Jesus' message suffered in so many allegedly Christian hands. When the Ghost Dance religion fell into decline in the early twentieth century, it had succeeded in realizing God's commission to Jack Wilson. Through his teaching, many Indian peoples found again the "road of life" as Indians, after their world had literally been taken from them.

4/New Tidings

Round Plain is a stretch of hay meadows cleared out of jackpine forest on the north side of the North Saskatchewan River, across from the small city of Prince Albert in Saskatchewan, Canada. A small Indian reserve, Sioux Wahpeton, occupies this land. Today, it has a commodious community building with a large gym, offices for the staff working for the Indian band, and rooms for social services. Scattered over the heath are small frame houses, the standard type constructed with Canadian government funds on Indian reserves. Wahpeton's band chief is a city-educated man active in the province-wide Federation of Saskatchewan Indian Nations. He shuttles between his office in the Federation's headquarters in Prince Albert and that in the Wahpeton band hall just out of sight of the city across the river. The band chief's daily driving back and forth over the Saskatchewan River bridge between reserve and city could symbolize the contemporary relationship between Canadian Indians and the national society, a visible separation carefully maintained in spite of continuing reliance on government fulfillment of its treaty obligations. Canadians see their society as an ethnic mosaic, and Sioux Wahpeton Reserve is a good place to observe this conception at work.

In the 1960s, Sioux Wahpeton Reserve was a piece of the Canadian mosaic hardly anyone saw. Ask someone in the street in Prince Albert, and chances were they had never heard of Sioux Wahpeton Reserve, though they probably could tell you how to get to Round Plain. Go out to the reserve, driving slowly along the winding sandy ruts that was the road, and you would find people living in homemade log cabins, no car but a buckboard wagon in the yard. Many of the people did not speak English. Those who wanted to earn something would hike the eight miles into Prince Albert to look for work, but often had to hike back at the end of the day penniless. At best, they might pick up a few days' wages as a farm laborer. Round Plain's sandy acres were poor for farming, its jackpine forest was good for nothing more valuable than firewood, it was much too small to support wild game, and it lacked a lake or stream for fishing. Welfare payments were the community's principal source of income.

Wahpeton Sioux on Round Plain are the descendants of refugees from the 1862 Minnesota Uprising, their people's last armed attempt to reclaim their country. The Wahpeton belong to the eastern branch of the Sioux, the Dakota; their language is a different dialect from that spoken by their western cousins, the Lakota. Their homeland in Minnesota was invaded by Euro-American colonists beginning in the 1830s, and by 1851 the Dakota were pressured to sign away, through a treaty, most of the state. Reservations assigned to them were deliberately made too small to sustain the people through hunting, so they would have no alternative but to farm.

August 1862 was a bad time for the Dakota. Monies promised them in the treaties of 1851 had gone mostly to pay debts the Euro-American traders claimed were owed them. When Dakota moved to their reservations in 1853 and 1854, they were faced with a determination by the Indian agents "to break up the community system among the Sioux: weaken and destroy their tribal relations; individualize them by giving each a separate home and having them subsist by industry—the sweat of their brows; till the soil; make labor honorable and idleness dishonorable; or, as it was expressed in short, *'make white men of them'*" (quoted in Prucha 1984:439). Crops in Minnesota did badly in 1862. The year before, most of the Indian agents and other government employees dealing with the Dakota had been replaced with a new and inexperienced set of men rewarded with these jobs for their loyalty to the political party that won the national elections of 1860. The Dakota lacked food in August 1862. Their regular annuity payments, set in their treaties, were held up, and local traders refused to sell them supplies on credit. One

Figure 20. Home of a member of the New Tidings congregation, Round Plain, Saskatchewan. A new government-built house stands before the log home formerly occupied.

trader was heard to remark, "If they are hungry, let them eat grass" (quoted in Prucha 1984:441).

On August 17, 1862, four Dakota impulsively murdered five colonists in Minnesota. Realizing the attack would stimulate retaliation, Dakota leaders quickly took the initiative and attacked the nearby Indian agency. Euro-American militia were mobilized, and President Lincoln in Washington released General John Pope from his engagement in the Civil War to march against the Dakota. Pope announced, "It is my purpose utterly to exterminate the Sioux if I have the power to do so. . . . Destroy everything belonging to them. . . . They are to be treated as maniacs or wild beasts, and by no means as people with whom treaties or compromises can be made" (quoted in Prucha 1984:443).

It is hardly to be wondered at that many Dakota fled north into Canada in 1862. Some hung around the little towns in Manitoba, just across the border from Minnesota; others slowly continued moving northwestward looking for work. By 1888, the Superintendent of the North-West Mounted Police detachment at Prince Albert in Saskatchewan reported:

> There are about 170 Sioux Indians living in the vicinity of Prince Albert, who have no treaty [with Canada], and obtain a living without the assistance of the Government. They came here from eleven to twelve years ago, and have since earned a precarious living by working about the towns and in the country, and by hunting. They are mostly Minnesota Sioux, who came into Canada after the massacre. For some time they lived about Oak Lake, Ellice and Qu'Appelle [in southern Manitoba and Saskatchewan], and gradually drifted here. A few are Tetons, who came with Sitting Bull in 1876 [to escape retribution after Custer's defeat at the Little Bighorn]. They now live in a small village on the north side of the Saskatchewan, near the Little Red River. They are hard working and moral. Some have expressed a wish to settle on a reserve, where they could engage in farming. Although so close to the town, they are all heathens and receive no Christian teaching whatever. (Perry 1889)

With such recommendations from its officials, the Canadian government in 1894 granted the immigrant Sioux around Prince Albert the small reserve at Round Plain. An agent's report in 1908 said Round Plain was the poorest reserve in his jurisdiction, suffering high mortality from tuberculosis. In 1913, there were sixty-six members of the Sioux Wahpeton band, and they earned what they could by selling berries, cut firewood, and hay. Five years later, in 1918, the worldwide influenza epidemic took the lives of a substantial number of the Round Plain community, so many, in fact, that few survivors could find spouses within their own band, and marriages with neighboring Cree Indians became common. The Cree have always lived in Canada and belong to the Algonkian stock, unrelated to Siouan. Cree are the largest Indian group in Saskatchewan, and in mixed marriages between Dakota and Cree, the children tend to identify with the Cree group and fail to learn the Dakota language and cultural tradition. Some Wahpeton Dakota sought spouses among the Assiniboin, another, although distinct, Siouan people of the Northern Plains.

The chief of Sioux Wahpeton Reserve, who has been active in the Federation of Saskatchewan Indian Nations, is a son of such a union; Dakota was not his first language, but he did grow up proud of his Wahpeton heritage.

Jack Wilson's religion came to Saskatchewan through evangelicals from the United States. Kicking Bear and Short Bull, the Lakota brothers-in-law who headed the "hostiles" outside Pine Ridge agency in December 1890, are credited by a Sioux Wahpeton band member, Sam Buffalo, with revealing knowledge of the religion to the Sioux, although Buffalo did not know whether they had themselves traveled to Saskatchewan. Lakota from Sitting Bull's band who had remained in Saskatchewan after their leader returned south were dancing the Ghost Dance on their reserve, Wood Mountain, in 1895. Sam Buffalo was told that sometime in the late 1890s, Saskatchewan Sioux gave up the active dancing that led exhausted participants into a trance, and the Dakota in Saskatchewan created a new form of the Ghost Dance religion incorporating the traditional Dakota Medicine Feast, much as the Pawnee were revitalizing their traditional rituals in the framework of Ghost Dance belief. The Dakota Medicine Feast brought together the owners of spiritually potent "medicine bundles" (sets of objects symbolic of spiritual blessing and, among the Dakota, often a variety of medicinal herbs as well). These people shared an ostentatiously generous feast served in treasured, polished heirloom wooden bowls in honor of their patron holy spirits, singing prayers and lighting braided bunches of sweetgrass for incense to express their gratitude to the Almighty and Its avatars. A little mound of earth in the middle of the floor represented the world, and a trail of red ocher paint going from east to west across it was the "good red path" or "road to life." The Ghost Dance version of this ceremony of "Prayer Singing" added songs derived from the Ghost Dance creed.

Fred Robinson came about 1900. He was an Assiniboin from Wolf Point, Montana, who had been a widower when he met a woman from an Assiniboin band in southern Saskatchewan. They married and lived on her reserve. She died, and Robinson took for his third wife a Dakota, Agnes, from Moose Woods (White Cap Reserve) near Saskatoon, Saskatchewan. Agnes was also widowed. She owned a well-built cabin and a herd of cattle at Moose Woods. Robinson moved into her home and helped her with the cattle. The Methodist Church was running a very active, model mission at Moose Woods then. Mrs. Robinson was a staunch communicant of that church, and Robinson's brother-in-law, whose house was only a few yards from his sister's, assisted the Methodists in the school they operated for the reserve children. Fred Robinson, much to his brother-in-law's disapproval, avoided the church.

Exactly when Fred Robinson was converted to the Ghost Dance religion is not known. It is known that in 1902 Robinson took instruction in Jack Wilson's religion from Kicking Bear, who had visited the prophet again that year. Moose Woods, where the favor of the Methodist missionary meant everything, was no place to preach a rival gospel, but at Round Plain Robinson found receptive ears. A gleam of his fervent evangelism comes through a letter preserved in a storage cellar Jack Wilson built beside his home in Mason Valley:

Moose Woods Reserve
Dundurn Jan 17/09

Jack Wilson

I thought I would write you a short letter today   I wil tell you who I am   Oct 27th 1905 you send me paint 3 can full and some medicine too   Jan 29th 1906 you wrote to me and send me (1 tomatoes can) full of paint. I tell you this so you can remember who I am   I am staying with the news you tell me all the time till now I have been as far north to a place called Prince Albert and I am telling them about the news and till now I am staying here for winter I came to this place and I am telling every day what they ought to do father will you help me with the heart of the people where the prayers come from I want you to help to make the people straight thought. Help me too   How can it be done to grow one church or prayer   Help me father that I want them to know forwards the road of life   Help me that I want the people on earth to think and go into the road of life   The people think they would have their own way and have good time, I am always talking about the everlasting life

Another thing is pulling the people and you know that I am telling them about the good road and good life and I am telling them too on one side the Bad road and the evil spirit   The last one I mention is a man have gone on that side you must hear that   There were not many people but this man he divides them into two and he spoil the whole thing   You know some people have good time. So he want it like that. He gave me some bad words and he send some to you, his name is Rufus Medicine. As it is hard to get the people in shape and I want you to quit them. The people here have raised $37.00 and send them to you as you have it already now   All the people that have paint [the holy red ocher] have raised money for you as what they say, and this fellow is going back to (poplar Mont[ana])   I am going to Prince Albert as they want me over there to tell them of the News. I will be back in few days again you seems to forget me so long so I write to you   You know me well so If you get this letter try and answer me

I am yours faithful worker

I shake hands with you with my Best thought

Fred Robinson

Rufus Medicine, like Robinson, married a Moose Woods woman, but seems to have lived only about two years on her reserve, spending most of his life at Brockton, Montana. He seems to have been a rival of Fred Robinson in leading the Ghost Dance religion in Saskatchewan. It was he who had mailed, in December 1908, the thirty-seven-dollar money order to Jack Wilson mentioned in Robinson's letter. Medicine wrote to Wilson on March 17, 1909, inquiring about the request for red ocher and white earth paints and magpie feathers, and finally on April 6 he received the three packages from Nevada. Fred Robinson's brother-in-law remembered that Rufus Medicine had returned to Moose Woods years later and died there, probably in the 1930s. Fred Robinson died of pneumonia at Moose Woods in November 1941, at about the age of eighty. In the 1960s, a handsome photograph of Robinson in Sioux costume hung prominently in the home of Henry Two Bears, then the leader of the Ghost Dance congregation at Round Plain.

"New Tidings" (*Woyaka Teca* in Dakota) is the name applied to Fred Robinson's version of Jack Wilson's teachings. Its origin is described in the gospel memorized by the Ghost Dance congregation leader. This is a portion of that gospel, recited in Dakota by the aged Mr. Two Bears on the Sioux Wahpeton Reserve in 1961, translated into English as he told it by his stepson Robert Goodvoice:

The New Tidings

Around 1890, there was a man by the name of Kicking Bear, who had a brother-in-law named Short Bull, with whom he was closely associated. Kicking Bear lost a daughter; she died; he roamed the plains, downhearted, unable to forget his loss. One night he saw a dream vision, stating that "all he worried about is known by Him Who gives power. There is a place where the dead souls gather." This he believed because it seemed to be *wakan* [holy].

He started off to find a spot where he could discover this, travelling through Montana to Nevada until he faced a mountain of rock. Halfway up was a house occupied by a human. Kicking Bear and Short Bull were welcomed by the occupant, all shaking hands. The occupant told them the purpose of their visit, saying, "You are looking for the soul of your deceased daughter; you firmly believe there is a place where souls gather. You are right."

This man was named Jack Wilson. He told them he could help them to see the deceased child among the souls. "You have to go further west, and there you will meet a bunch of people, a tribe, who have the power that they can enable you to see your child, a spirit in spirit-land. This group of people are overseers above the spirits, through the supervision of the Almighty Power. This tribe is the Thunderbirds, the mediators of the Almighty Power."

Jack Wilson had built a sweatlodge and placed in it sage. He laid Kicking Bear on the sage, covered him with a buffalo robe, and fanned him with an eagle fan. This put Kicking Bear into a trance, when he was able to go and see what Jack Wilson had promised him.

When, as he was in a trance, Kicking Bear approached the spirits' camp, he was walking on land. The camp was so big he couldn't see across it. He saw all his deceased relatives, father and mother, and among them his daughter. As far as he could see, the dwellings on both sides of him, left and right, had food (that is, meat), but none offered him food to eat. The dishes were wooden bowls (like those used for Medicine Feasts), no metal. He was satisfied, seeing his daughter and the tribe of spirits, and was about to return, when they said to him, "You've come this far, you might as well see the Creator, the Power that guides all things."

He was taken to see a Being, a Person who was very magnificent. This Person gave him a pipe and sweetgrass, and told him to stand upright and offer the pipe and grass to Him. He would then hear and answer them. The Creator thus confirmed the ancient way of praying to Him, and emphasized it was to be continued.

Another instruction Kicking Bear got was, "You thought your child had died and gone forever, but that's not the case. She has joined another tribe. When you rejoin your tribe on earth, tell the people, 'You are never happy when a person dies. You cut off your braids, and are downhearted. That's not pleasing to the

One Who gave them life.' When you get back to earth, take a ball of earth, dampen it, put it into the fire, and take it out. You will see it has turned perfectly red. Powder it and mark your face with it, as a token of happiness, pleasing to the Power." He told him, "When one of the earthly beings—the humans—passes away, leave them where they pass away, so their bones turn into dust. You make a scaffold and lay them up there; this is not right. The birds can eat them. The body comes from the earth, and there is where it should return. You should bury in the earth."

Now, as he was descending, it seemed to him that he was very near the sun. As he was coming down, he sang a song:

"I've come on high.
"The Father enabled me to beat that height."

There was nothing holding him as he was coming down, but he was floating slowly down like the eagle feather on the pipe he had been given. He had been told that when he returned to his people, they should dance to that song, with an eagle feather tied to their hair. That's where wearing eagle feathers on their head began.

When he awakened from this sleep, he was in the same place where he had started, with all these instructions and visions clearly remembered. When he awakened, he told his companions what he had seen. He had left out some things, which Jack Wilson put in, straightening out his dream for him. Apparently Jack Wilson had seen where he travelled.

Before this, when a family lost a member, some men would shove a sharpened stick through their flesh and leave it there, some women would cut themselves to show they were in mourning, for a year. Since Kicking Bear told of his dream, this kind of self-cruelty was done away with. Since then, they turned it into a kind of religious dance: on the seventh day, they gathered on a high hill and sang songs pertaining to what Kicking Bear had seen. Men and women joined in happiness, wearing the eagle feathers and the paint Kicking Bear had prepared.

The core of the New Tidings is the commandment to lead a "clean, honest life," as the Round Plain congregation put it. Believers prayed daily to the Almighty in gratitude and joy for the gift of life. The natural world shows forth the power and goodness of the Almighty. Followers of the New Tidings at Round Plain gathered regularly for many years to pray together, singing the holy songs reminding them of the prophets' journeys to the Almighty and the promise of eternal life in the Almighty's blessing. The congregation shared a communion feast of meat, corn, berries, and rice with raisins. (In Minnesota, the Dakota traditionally harvested wild rice.) Some members wore Ghost Dance shirts, not because they were thought to be bulletproof, but to help protect the wearer from evil temptations. Emphasis was on the "road of life," symbolized by the "good red path" of red ocher earth paint, east to west in the center of the room, and by the incense rising to heaven from the holy pipe and sweetgrass. Each communicant had a small personal "medicine bundle" symbolizing the good message of the New Tidings, to keep in the home and to carry to the prayer meetings where the bundles would be passed through the sweet incense smoke.

Sioux Wahpeton Reserve's New Tidings was an example of the real Ghost

Dance religion, a revitalization of tradtional—Dakota in this case—beliefs and ceremonies inspired by Jack Wilson's doctrine and the trance visions he led disciples into. The religion stimulated creative pruning of unobtainable or anachronistic elements, such as emphasis on bison, while incorporating effective new symbols. People in the small impoverished communities needed a creed that strengthened them to lead "clean, honest" lives that affirmed the goodness of their heritage and drew them together in mutual support. Active participants were mature men and women. Children observed their grandparents' daily morning prayers outdoors, hearing the pleas that the Almighty grant health and prosperity to families and friends, and growing in understanding of what is *wakan*, "holy." Parents used family mealtimes to discuss moral behavior in an edifying rather than dictatorial manner. Young people might heedlessly sow their wild oats, but as they became parents themselves, they would increasingly reflect upon life, seek the wisdom of older persons, and become more actively religious. The New Tidings, the "Holy Dance" prayer communions, were part of the living Dakota religion for twentieth-century Round Plain.

The Almighty Who sent the New Tidings was not a jealous god but the all-embracing Power of the universe. Whereas Christian denominations demanded that converts give up all other religious doctrines and practices, New Tidings reinforced Dakota tradition. New Tidings' incorporation of older Dakota beliefs, rituals, and symbols into Round Plain's "Sioux religion" was in the long run its vulnerable feature. By the late 1960s, younger people on the reserve no longer spoke Dakota. None of them were of exclusively Wahpeton ancestry, since the small size of the community—81 in 1963—had forced most of their parents to find spouses outside it. Without a school on the reserve, the children were immersed in English in the Prince Albert public schools. Although many young people could understand Dakota, and also Cree, they lacked fluency in speaking and this embarrassed them if they tried to talk about spiritual matters with their elders. The old people felt that the spiritual knowledge they had gained as Dakota could be properly imparted only in the Dakota language. Sam Buffalo tried, in 1971, to teach Dakota at Sioux Wahpeton Reserve; an anthropologist from the University of Saskatchewan helped him by getting information about Sioux language courses taught in the United States. Buffalo hoped that with the language, he might pass on New Tidings, but initial enthusiasm for learning Dakota died down, although some individuals have been learning it on their own, listening to tapes as well as to the old people. Neither New Tidings nor the older Dakota religion with which it had become inextricably linked could persist uninterrupted in the mixed heritages of the late-twentieth-century community.

Canadian Indian reserves changed considerably in the 1970s. Two events precipitated change: the appearance of the American Indian Movement (AIM) in Minnesota in 1968, and the publication of Prime Minister Trudeau's "White Paper" on Indian policy in 1969. For a decade, AIM challenged the United States Bureau of Indian Affairs and conservative Indian agents to yield greater political and economic autonomy to Indians. AIM leaders pointedly recalled the Minnesota Uprising and the troubles around Pine Ridge in 1890; Leonard Crow Dog, an Oglala activist in AIM, even revived the Ghost Dance ritual in 1973 and 1974. This "Red Power" movement frightened Canadian officials watching north of the border. Hoping to contain the movement to the United States, Prime Minister Trudeau announced a policy of ending the special legal status of Canadian Indians, extending to them the same rights and responsibilities, and no others, Euro-Canadians had. Trudeau thought the Indians wanted full inclusion in a Bill of Rights. To his surprise, Indians across Canada denounced the perfidy of the government in seeking to deny the treaty obligations it had incurred. Preservation of their special status under the treaties was their principal right, they asserted. They wanted self-determination, not assimilation. Hastily, the government retreated from the White Paper, pouring monies into the reserves to mollify the Indians.

Sioux Wahpeton Reserve exhibits the results of the Canadian government's anxiety during the 1970s over the dissatisfactions of the Indians. The reserve's commodious band hall with handsome facilities for sports, assemblies, and services is a monument to that anxiety. In the 1970s, frame houses replaced cabins, cars and pickups replaced buckboard wagons, a straight graded road led directly from the main highway to the reserve. The material improvements came through both direct assistance and indirect aid in the form of subsidized employment. Alongside the physical effects of a new governmental concern with Indians came Indian reassertion of the worth of their native heritages. Official and popular idealization of the cultural mosaic as uniquely Canadian gave the Indians, for the first time, an opening to argue the value and validity of Indian self-determination.

Until the 1970s, Indian children in Canadian schools, as in the United States, were generally forbidden to use their native languages and were taught that their cultures were inferior to European civilization. At last, after years of fighting by the Federation of Saskatchewan Indians (which did not add the word "Nations" to its title until the 1980s) and reserve parents, Indian communities gained input into their children's education. A few schools were given to reserve residents to administer, and more began classes in Indian languages and heritages. Such inclusion of Indian cultural materials in formal schooling signals acceptance of non-European peoples as equal in worth to Europeans, a revolution from nineteenth-century ideas. Indians' newly recognized legitimate pride in their cultures had a very concrete effect in Prince Albert. Until the 1960s, Indians in the city tended to stay on the side streets and to quietly give way on the sidewalks to Euro-Canadians. Now, the center of the city teems with Indians shopping, and they stride with confidence along the sidewalks.

In the dark nadir of Plains Indian societies toward the end of the nineteenth century, the Almighty reaffirmed the value of Indian cultures through Jack Wilson's holy message. Called New Tidings in Saskatchewan, the gospel carried the Dakota in bleak Round Plains through the decades when Euro-Canadians believed it was their "white man's burden" to wipe out Indian "savagery." Jack Wilson's doctrine of peaceable accommodation may seem passive, but it required a great deal of inner strength to preserve the core of an Indian culture against the massed onslaughts of government, missionaries, and invading colonists. Leading a "clean, honest life" instead of dropping by the wayside into alcoholism or despair was a difficult road for the besieged Indians of the days following their military defeats. Jack Wilson's road of life was a map to take Indian peoples through the decades when being Indian was treated as if it were a crime.

A century after the Sioux surrenders, the principles so beautifully enunciated in the Declaration of Independence are at last sinking into the consciousness of members of the dominant groups in the United States and Canada. Indians' inalienable rights to life, liberty, and the pursuit of happiness are recognized to be inviolable, whatever cultural tradition the Indian gives his or her allegiance. Accommodation is no longer the only road. With a political climate that admits Indians' human rights, there has come a renaissance of Indian cultures building on the cores guarded, in many instances, under Jack Wilson's creed. Now that the tide of conquest has ebbed in North America, tidings of a new road of life for Indians have become old. The Ghost Dance religion seems obsolete.

5/Black Elk Speaks

A renaissance in numbers and a renaissance in culture characterize American Indians in the late twentieth century. Indian populations double every generation now. Young people are the largest portion of these populations; like young persons everywhere, Indian youth wonder what is ahead in life, what kind of person they should try to become. "Apples"—red on the outside, white on the inside—disgust many. They are repelled by what they see as conventional, money-grubbing, plastic-loving, soul-less Americans. They look to "traditional Indian religion" for inspiration. Where, if they live in cities (half the Indian population does), can they find Indian religion?

Black Elk speaks to these uprooted Indians:

Today I send a voice for a people in despair.

You have given me a sacred pipe, and through this I should make my offering. . . . To the center of the world you have taken me and showed the goodness and the beauty and the strangeness of the greening earth, the only mother. . . . At the center of this sacred hoop you have said that I should make the tree to bloom. . . . It may be that some little root of the sacred tree still lives. Nourish it then, that it may leaf and bloom and fill with singing birds. Hear me, not for myself, but for my people; I am old. Hear me that they may once more go back into the sacred hoop and find the good red road, the shielding tree! (Neihardt [1932] 1961:279–280)

Beautiful words: They strike a chord in the hearts of Americans who long to affirm the unity of all life, long for loving communion in place of ruthless competition, for peace amidst nature in place of urban grubbiness. *Black Elk Speaks*, conveniently available in inexpensive paperback, became a favorite of the 1960s "counterculture," Americans who rejected what they judged to be the gross materialism of the majority. Some of the earnest seekers after beauty and goodwill and peace journeyed to South Dakota to find holy men like Black Elk to guide them.

Young Indians in the cities were touched by the country's growing dissatisfaction with "the Establishment," the institutions of government and education that seemed to propel the United States into a costly, ugly war in Vietnam. Some young urban Indians had strong ties to home reservations and visited frequently; others felt rootless, growing up in unstable homes with

Figure 21. Nicholas Black Elk. Photographed by Joseph Epes Brown, 1947.

parents confused by conflicts between urban American and rural Indian values. Many young Indians in cities do not look noticeably Indian and could blend into mainstream America, but is blending into the polyester crowd desirable? Indians who did appear racially distinct experienced discouraging discrimination. In the late 1960s, Indians in several cities organized citizen's action groups to pressure officials to improve living and employment conditions for Indians. Chippewa in Minneapolis called their group AIM, the

American Indian Movement. They had come together in AIM in 1966. By 1968, Minnesota Chippewa activists had reached out in alliance with dissatisfied Mohawk Iroquois in upstate New York calling themselves the Akwesasne Indian Nation. The national American Indian Movement was born.

By 1972, four years later, American Indians had staged a well-publicized occupation of abandoned Alcatraz Island in San Francisco Bay, had marched on Washington and publicly trashed offices in the Bureau of Indian Affairs, and were threatening what many claimed was a corrupt and unrepresentative tribal government on Pine Ridge Reservation. Parallel with but largely independent of the Vietnam War protest movement and of counterculture movements such as the Jesus People or Hare Krishna, AIM members and other militants searched for inspiration in Indian religion. They found *Black Elk Speaks*.

Black Elk Speaks was published in 1932 as "the Life Story of a Holy Man of the Oglala Sioux as told through John G. Neihardt (Flaming Rainbow)." John Neihardt, born in 1881 and raised in Nebraska, enjoyed the title Poet Laureate of Nebraska, bestowed on him by the state legislature in 1921 to honor his several books of poetry. Neihardt conceived a five-book epic poem on the United States settlement of the prairie West. To be named *A Cycle of the West*, it would tell of events from the "others' " point of view—the experiences of Indians and fur traders—as well as the view of homesteaders. Neihardt was no simple man of the soil pouring out his feelings in untutored meter: He became Professor of Poetry at the University of Nebraska in 1923, then literary editor of a major newspaper, the St. Louis *Post-Dispatch*, from 1926 to 1938. His works show a real gift for lyrical poetry and also his well-polished craftsmanship. *A Cycle of the West* was to be a grand work of literature, and deeply felt. It was to be historically true within a poet's license to flesh out bare facts.

To bring authenticity to his epic, Neihardt traveled to the scenes of historic events and interviewed aged people who had participated in or witnessed them. An Oglala named Nick Black Elk had been mentioned to Neihardt as someone who might be able to describe the Ghost Dance from the Lakota point of view. Neihardt needed this for the *Song of the Messiah* section of the *Cycle*. He went to Manderson, South Dakota, in August 1930 to find Nick Black Elk.

To Neihardt's surprise, Nick Black Elk "seemed to be expecting me and welcomed me as though he had seen me often" (DeMallie 1984:27). The "sphinx-like old chap," as Neihardt described him in a letter (*ibid.*), explained that he had come to feel he must record for all who might wish to read it, the vision he had experienced as a child, together with enough exposition of Lakota history and beliefs to render the vision intelligible. Black Elk spoke little English, indeed avoided using English (like Jack Wilson, or Henry Two Bears of Round Plain), so if he was to share his inspiring vision with more than just the Lakota people who could come to listen to him speak, he had to find a writer skilled in English. His son Ben Black Elk could translate from

Lakota to the everyday English he had learned attending Carlisle Indian School in Pennsylvania, but Ben was not much of a writer. Both Nick Black Elk and John Neihardt were convinced that a spiritual power had brought together the Lakota *wicaša wakan* and the Poet Laureate of Nebraska. Black Elk and several other elderly Lakota men spent several hours telling Neihardt what he wanted to know about the Ghost Dance and the Wounded Knee massacre, then Black Elk and Neihardt agreed that the poet would return the next summer to spend a much longer time recording the message of the *wicaša wakan*.

Neihardt wrote to the publisher of some of his books, William Morrow in New York, and obtained a contract for Black Elk's book, plus an advance payment to enable him to recompense Black Elk and his friends for their time with him. Most of this compensation was in the form of food for all who gathered at Nick Black Elk's home during the three weeks in May 1931 during which Neihardt listened to Black Elk speak. One memorable day, a couple hundred people attended a great feast at Neihardt's expense to mark the formal adoption of John Neihardt and his two daughters as kin to the Lakotas. John was named in Lakota *Peta Wigmunke*, "Flaming Rainbow," after the brilliant rainbow in Black Elk's childhood vision. Daughter Enid, who took down all Black Elk's translated words in stenographic shorthand, received the name *Sagye Wakan Yuha Mani Win*, "Woman Walks with Her Holy Stick" (her pencil?), and daughter Hilda was *Anpo Wicahpi Win*, "Daybreak Star Woman." Black Elk presented the Neihardts a handsome white canvas tipi painted with a flaming rainbow and other symbols of his vision.

Writing the book "is not a money-making scheme for me," Neihardt assured Black Elk. "I can make money faster and easier in other ways. I want to do this book because I want to tell the things that you and your friends know, and I can promise you that it will be an honest and a loving book" (DeMallie 1984:29). The Poet Laureate of Nebraska spoke all too true. Published in 1932 in the depth of the Great Depression, *Black Elk Speaks* sold so few copies that no royalty payment could be made. Not until the paperback edition came out in 1971, and the ninety-year-old Neihardt had been interviewed on the nationally televised "Dick Cavett Show," did the book begin to sell. Nick Black Elk had died in 1950, and John Neihardt would die in 1973, glimpsing at last the fulfillment of his collaborator's wish that his vision would reach the many who seek for spiritual truth.

Enid Neihardt's stenographic recording, taken down by the young woman sitting near her father in the warm May sun outside the Black Elk cabin, has been preserved. Other old Oglala men and Nick's son Ben made up the regular group around the Neihardts. Ben translated as his father spoke, and Enid wrote his words in her rapid shorthand. Back home the following month, Miss Neihardt transcribed and typed the record for her father to edit and polish. Comparison of the shorthand and typed transcription with the published version reveals the skill of John Neihardt in transforming the history of one Oglala man into the saga of a prophet—exactly what Nick Black Elk intended.

Figure 22. *Oglala community (Rosebud Reservation), early 1890s.*

Black Elk Speaks begins with a page entirely composed by Neihardt, informing readers that what they are about to peruse "is the story of all life that is holy and is good to tell, and of us two-leggeds sharing in it with the four-leggeds and the wings of the air and all green things; for these are children of the one mother and their father is one Spirit" (Neihardt [1932] 1961:1). These are Neihardt's words, not Black Elk's.

Enid Neihardt recorded that after introducing themselves by name, age, and place of birth, Black Elk and his friends Standing Bear, Fire Thunder, and Holy Black Tail Deer explained that the principal speaker was "the fourth of the name Black Elk. My father was a medicine man and was brother to several medicine men. My father was cousin to Crazy Horse's father" (DeMallie 1984:102). (Crazy Horse was a Sioux general at the Little Bighorn battle against Custer in 1876.) Then Nick Black Elk and his friends reminisced about the attitude of their people toward "the whites" and about events in their boyhood.

Black Elk recalled his first vision experience, when he was six years old, not long after he first rode a horse and was given a bow and arrows by his father. At this point in Enid's notes, Black Elk begins recounting the solemn vision he was vouchsafed over twelve days of unconsciousness when he was nine years old. When Black Elk had completed his account, Standing Bear corroborated the strange apparent coma of the boy and the change his companions saw in his character after he suddenly recovered. Enid Neihardt recorded a memoir of the life of Nick Black Elk, substantiated and expanded by his lifelong comrades. From time to time, Black Elk extrapolated general information, such as the legend of the origin of the holy pipe, printed on pages 3 to 5 of *Black Elk Speaks* but given much later in Black Elk's original account. John Neihardt similarly created a conjunction between passages on Lakota attitudes toward Euro-Americans and Black Elk's memories, mentioned days later that May, when the old man talked of his travels with Buffalo

Bill's Show. What Black Elk actually spoke, as Ben Black Elk translated, was a more or less chronological narrative of the events and topics, principally battles, that typically interested Lakota men who grew up in the late nineteenth century. What John Neihardt published was transmuted into an art form in the European literary tradition.

Nine-year-old Black Elk's "great vision," as Neihardt referred to the twelve-day experience, is the heart of *Black Elk Speaks*. It was the impetus to Nick Black Elk's sense of mission leading him to present his memoir orally to John and Enid Neihardt. For a nine-year-old Lakota boy, especially a child of a family of *wapiyapi* (healers, including those, the *wicaša wakan* type, relying primarily on spiritual healing methods), to spontaneously experience a mystical vision was not particularly unusual, but Black Elk's vision was considerably longer than would be expected in a child. When he first recovered from his traumatic vision, Black Elk would not reveal it to anyone. He pondered it for years, until, as he was reaching young manhood, he felt more and more troubled by his failure to obey the call of the holy beings. Noticing their son's malaise, his parents asked a *wicaša wakan* to talk with the youth. As was customary for the Sioux—and in most societies that recognize visions as a source of knowledge—an older, practiced spiritual leader normally interpreted (or as Henry Two Bears put it, "straightened out") a novice's images.

Figure 23. Women drying beef, outside a typical Oglala home, Rosebud Reservation, early 1890s.

Young Black Elk's mentor, Black Road, authenticated the vision and instructed him in carrying out one of its recommended devotions, the Horse Dance. This was a major Lakota public ceremony in which a *wicaša wakan* invoked spiritual power to bless and make healthy the entire community. The power invoked was so strong that celebrants' horses walked solemnly and then danced of their own accord, it seemed, without conscious guidance from the men who sat on them. Aided by his parents, Black Road, and several other older men, Black Elk successfully led the required set of mounted men and young women through the exciting ritual, reenacting, he realized, much of his elaborate vision. When they finished, many people came up to thank him for bringing them good fortune, and he was received into the company of *wicaša wakan*.

Black Elk's career as a *wicaša wakan* followed a conventional course. He went out alone as a supplicant seeking greater spiritual power through additional visions, and he was rewarded by seeing that he was given power to cure and the obligation to perform the *heyoka* ceremony demonstrating this gift. At the age of nineteen, Black Elk began accepting pleas to cure the ill; their grateful relatives gave him horses when his patients recovered. (He ruefully mentioned to the Neihardts that it had not yet become customary to give a *wapiyapi* money to recompense his work in healing.) In *Black Elk Speaks*, Neihardt ([1932] 1961:207) has Black Elk say, "Of course I would have done it for nothing," but does not add that he would have been scandalized if a patient's family had neglected to materially demonstrate their gratitude.

Black Elk was twenty-three in 1886, earning a reputation among his people as a healer but still single and eager to "see the great water, the great world and the ways of the white men; this is why I wanted to go [with Buffalo Bill Cody's Wild West Show]. So far I looked back on the past and recalled the people's ways. . . . I got disgusted with the wrong road that my people were doing now. . . . I made up my mind I was going away from them to see the white man's ways. If the white man's ways were better, why I would like to see my people live that way" (DeMallie 1984:245).

With about one hundred other Indians, both men and women, including about ten of his Oglala friends, Black Elk traveled via Omaha and Chicago to New York. For three months, the Indians performed mock battles and dances in Madison Square Garden. In March 1887, Black Elk went with the show to England, took part in a command performance before Queen Victoria and her court, and continued in the regular public shows in London, Manchester, and Birmingham for an entire year. Black Elk told the Neihardts the Queen had said to the Indians as she congratulated them for their performances, "I wish that I had owned you people, for I would not carry you around as beasts to show to the people" (DeMallie 1984:250). Neihardt toned this down to, "If you belonged to me, I would not let them take you around in a show like this" (Neihardt [1932] 1961:225).

Other lines were made more dramatic in Neihardt's version of Black Elk's memoir. Black Elk had actually said that he and his Oglala comrades in the show "were out there for adventure" (DeMallie 1984:248), that he went to see the world and whether the "white man's ways were better," as any young man might wonder. Neihardt, however, had him say, "I even thought that if the Wasichus [white men] had a better way, then maybe my people should live that way. I know now that this was foolish, but I was young and in despair" (Neihardt [1932] 1961:219). In the Poet Laureate's version, Black Elk's very human youthful eagerness for adventure, tempered by an open mind for wisdom wherever he might find some, was subtly excised in favor of a mythical personage driven by anguish to desert his people, to seek fruitlessly for means of salvation. "I felt that my people were just altogether lost," Black Elk said, "because I was a long way from home" (DeMallie 1984:246). Neihardt did not give us this homesick youth; instead, he made the emotion tragic: "I was like a man who had never had a vision. I felt dead and my people seemed lost and I thought I might never find them again" (Neihardt [1932] 1961:221). Black Elk explained to Neihardt that he did no healing at that time but "was among other men just as a common man" (DeMallie 1984:247). His homesickness gave way as his friends urged him to go with them and the show to England. Remembering how he sang before the Queen, he exclaimed, "This was the most happy time!" (DeMallie 1984:251). Neihardt dropped the exclamation point Enid had recorded: "That was a very happy time" (Neihardt [1932] 1961:227). And Neihardt closed poignantly, "We liked Grandmother England [Victoria]. . . . Maybe if she had been our Grandmother, it would have been better for our people" (*ibid.*). That was not what Black Elk spoke.

John Neihardt did not know that two letters written, in Lakota, by Black Elk from Europe had been printed in the *Iapi Oaye*, a Lakota-language monthly newspaper published by the Dakota Indian Mission of the Presbyterian and Congregational Churches. These letters show the young man seeking wisdom. In February 1888, Black Elk told the folks back home, "So my relatives, the Lakota people, now I know the white men's customs well. One custom is very good. Whoever believes in God will find good ways—that is what I mean. . . . I have stayed here three [actually, two] years. And I am able to speak some of the white men's language" (DeMallie 1984:8–9).

Returning to the reservation in the fall of 1889, Black Elk published an account of his search for spiritual guidance among the whites, again writing in Lakota in the *Iapi Oaye*:

> My relatives, I am Lakota. . . . [O]f the white man's many customs, only his faith, the white man's beliefs about God's will, and how they act according to it, I wanted to understand. I traveled to one city after another, and there were many customs around God's will. 'Though I speak with the tongues of men and of angel . . . [here Black Elk quotes the entire first verse of I Corinthians, chapter 13, from the New Testament]. So Lakota people, trust in God! Now all along I trust in God. I work honestly and it is good; I hope the people will do likewise. . . . Across the big ocean is where they killed Jesus; again I wished to see it but it was four days

on the ocean and there was no railroad. If horses go there they died of thirst. Only those long-necks (camels) are able to go there. (It would require) much money for me to be able to go over there to tell about it myself. (DeMallie 1984:9–10)

In his half a year in New York and two full years in Europe—England, Germany, Italy, and France—Black Elk had ample opportunity to observe "white men." He and two friends had missed the boat when Buffalo Bill's show returned home from England, and the three Indians then signed up with a rival Wild West show on tour. Black Elk eventually became ill and was befriended by a young Parisienne whose parents hospitably allowed him to live with the family. When Buffalo Bill opened his show in Paris in 1889, Black Elk went to see him, was welcomed with a dinner in his honor, and was generously given the pay owed from the previous year, plus a ticket home when he admitted he wanted to return rather than rejoin the show.

Back on Pine Ridge Reservation, Black Elk got a job as a store clerk, and in 1892 married Kate War Bonnet. Black Elk had participated with other *wicaša wakan* in the Ghost Dance during 1889–1890 and had resumed his practice as a healer. Somewhat reluctantly, he fought with other Lakota, assisting the Miniconjou fired upon at Wounded Knee Creek. That disaster so angered him that he retreated to Kicking Bear's camp on the naturally fortified butte and rode out from there with other young men to gain revenge, fighting once with a troop of soldiers and a second time being forcibly restrained by his companions from a foolhardy sally against cavalry. The decision of the chiefs, Red Cloud and Young Man Afraid of His Horses (full translation, Young Man of Whom the Enemy is Afraid Even of His Horses), to surrender rather than continue fighting through the harsh winter, sat hard with Black Elk, who was slightly mollified by being selected one of the four "great warriors" to lead the procession of Lakota to the surrender ceremony at the agency. Black Elk concluded his account of these years to Neihardt with the line, "Two years later I was married" (DeMallie 1984:282).

Neihardt's version of the ending of Black Elk's account leaves out the young man's hot hunger for revenge and his terse statement of finally accepting the responsibilities of maturity, "Two years later I was married." Neihardt concludes the narrative of the Lakotas' arrival at the Pine Ridge agency in January 1891 with these words of his own, not Black Elk's:

And so it was all over.
    I did not know then how much was ended. When I look back now from this high hill of my old age, I can still see the butchered women and children lying heaped and scattered all along the crooked gulch as plain as when I saw them with eyes still young. And I can see that something else died there in the bloody mud, and was buried in the blizzard. A people's dream died there. It was a beautiful dream.
    And I, to whom so great a vision was given in my youth—you see me now a pitiful old man who has done nothing, for the nation's hoop is broken and scattered. There is no center any longer, and the sacred tree is dead. (Neihardt [1932] 1961:276)

Tragic epiphany—but what Black Elk actually said to John Neihardt at that point was anything but the end of an epic. Nick Black Elk said:

You have heard what I have said about my people. I had been appointed by my vision to be an intercessor of my people with the spirit powers and concerning that I had decided that sometime in the future I'd bring my people out of the black road into the red road [of life]. From my experience and from what I know, and in recalling the past from where I was at that time, I could see that it was next to impossible, but there was nothing like trying. . . .

At that time I could see that the hoop was broken and all scattered out and I thought, "I am going to try my best to get my people back into the hoop again." At this time, when I had these things in my mind, I was abroad with strange people. [In other words, this period of soul-searching and apprehension of the blackness of the Lakotas' road was the time of his peregrinations in Europe, well before Wounded Knee.] . . . At that time the wilds were vanishing and it seemed the spirits altogether forgot me and I felt almost like a dead man going around—I was actually dead at this time, that's all [he means that his healing power had left him while he was away from his homeland]. In my vision they had predicted that I was chosen to be intercessor for my people so it was up to me to do my utmost for my people and everything that I did not do for my people, it would be my fault—if my people should perish it seemed that it would be my fault. If I were in poverty my people would also be in poverty, and if I were helpless or died, my people would die also. But it was up to me to scheme a certain way for myself to prosper for the people. If I prosper, my people would also prosper.

I am just telling you this, Mr. Neihardt. You know how I felt and what I really wanted to do is for us to make that tree bloom. On this tree [of life] we shall

Figure 24. After the battle, Wounded Knee, 1890. This devastation and defeat became the popular image perpetuated by Neihardt's book.

Figure 25. Oglala arrived for a treaty council, 1889.

Figure 26. Brulé Lakota Sioux men gathered at Rosebud agency, 1894. The men seated at the far left carry ceremonial pipes and eagle-feather fans for an invocation to bless the gathering. Crow Dog and Two Strike, two of the "hostile" leaders of January 1891, stand in right center with their Brulé friends.

prosper. Therefore my children and yours are relative-like [kin] and therefore we shall go back into the hoop and here we'll cooperate and stand as one. . . . Our families will multiply and prosper after we get this tree to blooming. (DeMallie 1984:293–294)

Hardly a "pitiful old man" speaking. Black Elk had at last figured out a scheme to lead his people onto the road of life. John Neihardt would publish his vision and help him make a film about Lakota beliefs, so that all the thousands of Lakota would learn of the spirits' promise to bless the people. Euro-Americans, too, would come to know the happy destiny of the Lakota, and through the Neihardt family could assist the Indian people. After decades of groping in discouragement, the Lakota would be energized by Black Elk's prophecy: As he himself prospered through his collaboration with John Neihardt, they would find means to prosper. Black Elk saw the tree of life blooming once more for the Lakota; "you remember," he said to Neihardt, "I saw many happy faces behind those six grandfathers" in the vision (DeMallie 1984:294).

What had Black Elk been doing all those years between 1892 and 1930?

Apparently, John Neihardt never realized that for a substantial portion of his adult life, Nick Black Elk had been employed as a catechist for the Roman Catholic mission on Pine Ridge Reservation. He had probably been baptized into the Episcopal Church when he joined the Buffalo Bill Cody Wild West Show, since this was a condition required of all the Indian performers. (Their "moral welfare" was supervised by an Episcopal minister kept on the payroll of the show for that purpose.) Judging from his letters published in *Iapi Oaye*, Black Elk's experiences in Europe had confirmed his acceptance of Christianity. Kate Black Elk had been a Catholic when they married, and the couple's children were baptized in that church. Kate died about 1903, leaving her husband the full responsibility for their two surviving little boys, John and Ben.

Accepting Christianity did not imply to Black Elk that he must abjure all Lakota beliefs. If there is one omnipotent God in Christian doctrine, and a universal Power in Lakota cosmology, there seemed to the Lakota a fundamental agreement between the religions; a Lakota had only to add knowledge of Jesus Christ, whose historical existence the Lakota happened not to have learned of earlier, to Lakota belief to say he or she had accepted Christianity. Late in 1904, Black Elk was treating an ill child through the spirits invoked in the *yuwipi* ritual. A Jesuit priest from the Pine Ridge mission strode into the tent. According to Black Elk's daughter Lucy, the man seized the tobacco offerings to the spirits and threw them into the stove, grabbed Black Elk's drum and rattle and hurled them outside the tent, and shook Black Elk himself

Figure 27. Page 63, *Oglala men enjoying the Grass Dance (now known as the men's traditional dance at powwows), Rosebud Reservation, early 1890s.*

Figure 28. Page 63, *Oglala women enjoying the Round Dance, Rosebud Reservation, 1889.*

Figure 29. Page 63, *Oglala family and friends about to feast in honor of young women come of age, Rosebud Reservation, 1892.*

Figure 27

Figure 28

Figure 29

by the neck, proclaiming, "Satan, get out!" Lucy explained, "My father . . . knew a little English so he walked out" (Steinmetz 1980:158). The priest gave the Catholic sacraments to the ill child and prayed with him, then left the tent and ordered Black Elk, sitting outside, "Come on and get in the buggy with me" (*ibid.*). Black Elk obeyed, and for two weeks took instruction in the Catholic faith at Holy Rosary Mission. On December 6, 1904, he was baptized with the name of Nicholas, the date being St. Nicholas Day.

What is particularly interesting about the 1904 conversion is that on a previous occasion, in 1902, a similar incident had occurred. At that time, a Jesuit had interrupted Black Elk's *yuwipi* curing by desecrating all his paraphernalia, but in that incident Black Elk triumphed: The priest soon afterward fell from his horse and died, and Black Elk's patient recovered. Why, two years later, was Black Elk so ready to give up his calling as a *wapiyapi* and accept full conversion to Christianity? Black Elk told Neihardt that he had grown increasingly anxious over a second power given him in his great vision, the power to cause holocaust through a secret herb from the Black Hills. Neihardt omitted the description of this "war herb" from his retelling of the vision; he recounted only the gift of the healing power. By rejecting his Lakota religion, Black Elk felt he was safely rejecting the destructive power that had been given him in tandem with healing. Perhaps, also, Kate's death undermined his faith in his Lakota power.

Exhibiting such quick understanding and zeal as a Catholic that the mission made him a catechist in 1907, Black Elk began giving instruction and Bible readings. (The Gospel and Epistles of the New Testament had been translated into Lakota, and the Jesuits had prepared a picture catechism called *The Two Roads*. Native catechists could work in their own language.) As a catechist, he was paid five dollars per month, and when an ordained priest could not be present—which happened regularly in the isolated reservation communities served by circuit-riding mission priests—Black Elk led Sunday services. He was also a leader in the Catholic men's organization, the St. Joseph Society, and his second wife, Anna, had a parallel role in the Catholic women's group, the St. Mary Society. (Anna had been a widow when she married Nick in 1906, and she bore their daughter Lucy that year and another son, Nick, Jr., in 1914.) The Black Elk home was a center for Catholic counseling and worship.

Nick and Anna Black Elk were so highly regarded by the Jesuits at Holy Rosary Mission that they were sent, with another Lakota couple, as missionaries to the Arapaho, to the Winnebago, and, accompanying a priest, to the Sisseton Dakota. The Black Elks returned home after a month or two of working with each of these foreign peoples, much to the disappointment of the Jesuits, although in their own view the Black Elks had been successful in organizing the Indians to accept Catholic teaching and had no reason to remain away from Pine Ridge longer. Nick Black Elk attended the 1907 annual Catholic Indian Congress as well as a national congress for Catholic missions, reporting them, in Lakota, in the mission newspaper: "I went to a large meeting of white men in Indianapolis, Indiana. . . . Truly I saw how they were able to trust in God; truly, because they live with God, peace dwells with them. Therefore, my relatives, show respect to the priests who live with you and obey them, and hold on to what they tell you and stand firm. Thus peace will be with you, too" (DeMallie 1984:17).

The stipend paid to Indian catechists was insufficient for a family to live on, so Black Elk supported himself and his dependents by farming. Mission records mention that in 1909, Nick Black Elk was due to receive eighty head of cattle. By 1912, however, Black Elk had been diagnosed as suffering from tuberculosis, the worst health scourge on the reservation. He went to Hot Springs for treatment, but never fully recovered from the disease, and his lessened capacity for manual labor was exacerbated by partial blindness. This blindness was said to have been the result of miscalculation of a trick he used in his *yuwipi* curing ritual. In common with other *wicaša wakan* he honestly believed spirits came to the ritual when he invoked them, but as was customary, he considered it necessary to impress lay persons with the power of the invisible spirits by clothing them in a scary magic show. He surreptitiously would put a pinch of gunpowder in the fire to cause a brilliant flare-up, and once the explosion caused a shower of sparks that damaged his eyes. By 1917, he had to take his son Ben out of Carlisle Indian School because, he said, he could no longer farm without help.

"Black Elk is an efficient Catechist, but like many fullbloods a very poor manager," remarked one of the Jesuits at the mission. "He will always be a beggar, no matter how much money one would give him. . . . He never has anything and always asks for something. Poor fellow! And yet he can do a great deal and has done much in the past" (DeMallie 1984:22–23). Another priest advised against sending "Uncle Nick" money he had requested: "Begging has become a passion with many of these fellows" (DeMallie 1984:20). These priests failed to understand Lakota values. The "passion for begging" was an earnest invitation by Lakota to their Euro-American friends to use the traditional avenue of generosity to establish leadership. Only by freely giving to fellow Lakota all he received could Black Elk earn respect as a true leader. His success as a catechist depended on his fulfilling the traditional role of the wise leader, always marked in Lakota society by generosity to the point of impoverishing oneself.

Black Elk's preaching as well as his ministering to the troubled or needy was much praised. One Jesuit said Nick Black Elk had been responsible for at least four hundred conversions to Catholicism among his people. The Black Elks were invited, in 1926, to live in a house built by the mission for an Indian catechist in the reservation community called Oglala. Well known by then, Nick Black Elk was probably the unidentified Indian photographed on top of Mount Rushmore at the dedication of its monumental carvings of the four presidents, in 1925. Black Elk was performing in summer "Indian shows" put on for tourists in the Black Hills. His other side was photographed in about 1910, wearing a dark three-piece suit with white shirt and a tie, holding out a rosary with a crucifix to his little daughter Lucy standing before him with her hands in the attitude of Christian prayer. This photograph was used in

1925 on the cover of a fund-raising publication of the Bureau of Catholic Indian Missions. The next year, the Bureau used a drawing based on the photograph, but put Black Elk into Indian costume of buckskins and feather bonnet. Black Elk was back in 1935 in a restaging of the 1910 photograph, a new little girl taking the place of the now-grown Lucy. The 1935 photograph was used during the 1940s by Holy Rosary Mission as a symbol of their efforts with the Lakota.

John Neihardt's first interpreter on Pine Ridge Reservation in 1930 had warned him that Black Elk might not talk to him about the Ghost Dance and the old beliefs. The reason was not that Nick Black Elk was antagonistic to Euro-Americans, but that he had for so many years put the old religion behind him. Neihardt's first interpreter knew Black Elk well because they were both catechists for the Catholic faith. Another Lakota catechist, who played the organ in the Manderson community church where Black Elk worshipped, said, "He never talked about the old ways. All he talked about was the Bible and Christ" (Steinmetz 1980:159). Black Elk's decision to tell John Neihardt about his "great vision" and traditional Lakota beliefs was as radical as his 1904 conversion to Roman Catholicism. Was it decade after decade of poverty and illness on the reservation that persuaded Black Elk that strict adherence to Christianity was not the road of life? Black Elk never explained his reconversion, and John Neihardt, unaware he was listening to a prominent Catholic catechist, did not ask.

Black Elk Speaks has such wide appeal, both to non-Indians and to Indians living in the midst of Euro-American society, not simply because John Neihardt infused a mythic flavor into Black Elk's story. Black Elk himself created a universal religion grounded in Lakota beliefs but resonating with Christian symbols. No less than Jack Wilson, Nick Black Elk was a prophet. John Neihardt was Black Elk's apostle, the Paul to his Jesus, one might say. A major difference between Jack Wilson and Nick Black Elk was that Wilson's revitalization movement took hold quickly, disciples fanning out across the West igniting the movement among dozens of Indian peoples. Black Elk's gospel seemed stillborn. It took the 1960s counterculture movement to discover the message in the inexpensive paperback reprint of the thirty-year-old book published by the Poet Laureate of Nebraska.

Holy Rosary Mission had been shocked when its priests saw *Black Elk Speaks* in 1932. The Jesuits had had no reason to suspect Nick Black Elk of harboring continuing faith in his ancestral beliefs. To appease his friends among the priests, Black Elk wrote, in January 1934:

> I told about the people's ways of long ago and some of this a white man put in a book but he did not tell about current ways. Therefore I will speak again, a final speech.
>
> Now I am an old man. . . . For the last thirty years I have lived very differently from what the white man told about me. I am a believer. The Catholic priest Short Father [Joseph Lindebner, S.J.] baptized me thirty years ago. From then on they have called me Nick Black Elk. Very many of the Indians know me. . . . I say in my own Sioux Indian language, [the] "Our Father". . . . I believe in the seven

sacraments of the Catholic Church. . . . I participated in the retreat for catechists.
. . . All my family is baptized. . . . I send my people on the straight road that
Christ's church has taught us about. While I live I will never fall from faith in
Christ. (DeMallie 1984:59–60)

The same year, 1935, that Black Elk sat for the restaged photograph of
himself offering the rosary and crucifix to an Oglala child, he took a job in
a Sioux pageant staged three times each day during the summer season by a
businessman of Rapid City, the center of Black Hills tourism. Black Elk
supervised much of the organization of the show and performed in it himself,
dancing and going through several rituals, including offering the pipe to the
Almighty and drumming, rattling, and singing his old healing prayers over a
pretend patient. This was a secular show. That Black Elk dared to casually
go through what he once believed to be potent rituals suggests that his letter
of 1934 affirming his Catholicism was sincere.

Late in November 1944, John Neihardt and his daughter Hilda came to
Pine Ridge Reservation to research a history of the Oglala. Neihardt was
employed then by the Bureau of Indian Affairs. For seven days in December,
Neihardt again interviewed Black Elk, Hilda Neihardt serving as stenographer
while another Lakota Catholic catechist interpreted for Black Elk. The 1944
material, all traditional history, legends, and customs, Neihardt published in
1951 as *When the Tree Flowered* (referring to Black Elk's "great vision" of
a flowering tree representing pre-reservation Lakota life). (For text of 1944
interview material, see DeMallie 1984.) This book makes no comment on the
principal teller's personal beliefs. Meanwhile, between the recording of the
material and its publication in *When the Tree Flowered*, a young man named
Joseph Epes Brown, who had read *Black Elk Speaks*, made a pilgrimage to
Pine Ridge to meet the *wicaša wakan*. Over the winter of 1947–1948, and the
summers of 1948 and 1949, Brown lived at Manderson and, at Black Elk's
request, recorded "the seven rites of the Oglala Sioux." Ben Black Elk was
the interpreter for his father, as he had been with the Neihardts in 1931.
Joseph Epes Brown published in 1953 what Black Elk spoke to him as *The
Sacred Pipe*.

Brown's book is second only to *Black Elk Speaks* as a contemporary bible
of Indian religion. It is the key to Black Elk as the prophet of a revitalization
movement. Black Elk systematized Oglala religion. Only in *The Sacred Pipe*
is that religion ordered into seven sacramental rites, in parallel with Roman
Catholicism. Black Elk and Brown consistently refer the reader to other
parallels between Lakota and Christian religions. The "red road" in Sioux
ritual symbolism is explained in a footnote to be similar to the vertical element
of the Cross, to the "straight and narrow way" in Christian thought, and to
an Islamic symbol (Brown 1953:7). John Neihardt cast Black Elk's words into
a mythic mode; Joseph Brown, who became a professor of religious studies
at the University of Montana, framed them in scholarly comparisons. *The
Sacred Pipe* directly addresses Euro-Americans wishing to understand an
Indian religion:

We have been told by the white men, or at least by those who are Christian, that God sent to men His son, who would restore order and peace upon the earth; and we have been told that Jesus the Christ was crucified, but that he shall come again at the Last Judgment, the end of this world or cycle. This I understand and know that it is true, but the white men should know that for the red people, too, it was the will of *Wakan-Tanka*, the Great Spirit, that an animal turn itself into a two-legged person in order to bring the most holy pipe to His people; and we too were taught that this White Buffalo Cow Woman who brought our sacred pipe will appear again at the end of this "world," a coming which we Indians know is now not very far off. . . . We Indians know the One true God, and . . . we pray to Him continually.* (Black Elk in Brown 1953:xix–xx)

A lifetime of reflection upon the religions he had been taught, the Lakota and the Christian, had given Black Elk the insight that both his people and the Europeans were children of the Almighty. God sent an incarnation of *wakan*, "holiness," to each people: to the Europeans a perfect young man, to the Lakota a perfect young woman. Each incarnation presented the people with a powerful symbol through which to worship: Jesus, the Cross; White Buffalo Cow Woman, the Pipe. Cross and Pipe are closely similar, each a wooden shaft representing the Tree of Life. God made the world and made it good, and gave it to humans and other forms of life, who fulfill God's will if they live together in peace and goodwill. This Christian message is, if anything, more clear in the Lakota version, for whereas the historical persecution and execution of Jesus bloodies the European gospel, the Lakota preserves the focus on goodness by telling how the would-be persecutor, a man wanting to rape the beautiful woman alone on the prairie, crumbles into ashes as he is about to violate the incarnation. Her final epiphany is as the glorious pure, white bison running free over the sweet-smelling flowery prairie.

Black Elk—Hehaka Sapa in his own Lakota language—and Jack Wilson, Wovoka the Paiute, were born only three years apart, 1863 and 1860. Both were young boys when Euro-American colonists invaded their homelands; both experienced the military conquest of their people and their assignment to reservations. Both were sons of respected native doctors and themselves successful doctors in their peoples' traditions. Both Jack Wilson and Nick Black Elk were taught Christianity. One was inspired to preach a doctrine of superficial accommodation to contemporary circumstances and deep commitment to the Indian community, and sparked an immediate revival among dozens of Indian groups; he lived out his life as a Paiute doctor. The other seemed to forsake his Indian religion and espoused Roman Catholicism, working for three decades leading Lakota Christian congregations. Strangely, it was Nick Black Elk who years after his death brought Indian religion to thousands of Americans of Indian ancestry and even to non-Indians.

Precisely because Black Elk was a trained Christian catechist, he could create a synthesis linking Lakota symbols to Christian parallels, making them

* From *The Sacred Pipe: Black Elk's Account of the Seven Rites of the Oglala Sioux*, Recorded & Edited by Joseph Epes Brown. Copyright © 1953 by the University of Oklahoma Press.

intelligible to people who grew up in Euro-American society. Jack Wilson spoke to men and women whose thinking had been formed wholly within Indian cultures, in Indian languages. Hundreds of thousands of American Indians in the United States at present have English as their first language, have had formal schooling, and are familiar with city living. Now many of them want to recover their Indian heritage. Jack Wilson's sketchy gospel in Mooney's monograph does not tell them enough, and the doctor can no longer send tomato cans of holy red paint to sustain personal relationships wtih disciples. Black Elk deliberately expounded Lakota belief in detail to instruct foreigners. Today, a century after Indian autonomy was crushed and Indian children were deprived of the full experience of their ancestral cultures, his books can serve, as Sioux writer Vine Deloria, Jr. (1979), notes, as an "Indian Bible."

Black Elk was fortunate in working with two exceptionally able collaborators. Meeting John Neihardt was partly a coincidence, for Neihardt might have engaged a different interpreter at Pine Ridge who would perhaps have taken him to another old man for information. It was Neihardt's book, however, that brought Joseph Brown to Black Elk. Neihardt's lyrical style and bent for epic myth made Black Elk an iconic figure of the tragic prophet. Brown's scholarly propensities filled out and reinforced the prophet's message. Black Elk's genius lay in organizing Lakota religion according to a Christian framework, emphasizing characteristics amenable to expression in symbols reminiscent of Christian symbols, yet keeping a Lakota essence. His teaching is as valid as that of any other *wicaša wakan* recognized by Lakota communities, since the religion accepts ongoing personal revelations and has no fixed, immutable written dogma.

Still, Black Elk's teachings are far from the whole of Lakota beliefs and practices. Black Elk omitted the popular trickster figure Iktomi ("Spider"), except for a brief mention in the Falling Star myth in Neihardt's 1944 book. The seven sacraments in *The Sacred Pipe* do not include the *heyoka* ceremony, which most Sioux would consider a major element in their repertoire of worship. Of the mysteries expressed through animal figures, there is only White Buffalo Cow Woman. Black Elk may have thought Iktomi too picaresque to carry a religious message. *Heyoka*, in which the *wakan* participants communicate their otherworldly nature through strange, magical, and clowning acts, no doubt seemed to Black Elk beyond the comprehension of Christians as he knew them. Animal mysteries he had seen derided as pagan polytheism. Particularly in *The Sacred Pipe*, he chose those elements of Lakota religion that his experience suggested would not jar the sensibilities of Euro-Americans. His mission was to make it easy for those who knew only Judaeo-Christian religions to recognize and respect Lakota religion as a true religion. It was, ironically, those many years of intimate living with Europeans and the Catholic mission that enabled Black Elk to speak effectively for Indian religion today. He was the same age as Jack Wilson, but he spoke to later generations.

6/Wounded Knee Again

The American Indian Movement was started by a group of men that had been living in an urban situation. . . . They first started to work in the way of many urban organizations to try to gain control of a portion of Federal Government spending. They demanded that the Indian people be given a share so that they could begin working towards a solution to their problems. . . . The American Indian Movement worked in Minneapolis for its first year and people who found out what a tremendous help it was for the American Indian people started spreading the word of it. Of course, during its origin, the leaders of the American Indian Movement knew that there was something missing. . . . At that time, some of the American Indian Movement leaders heard about a spiritual leader on the Rosebud Sioux Reservation named Crow Dog and they made a trip down there to Rosebud to visit with Crow Dog and see if they could gain some sort of spiritual direction that they had realized was so vitally missing.

And Crow Dog told them that if they were to be a true Indian organization, they had to have the spiritual involvement of our medicine men and our holy people. And that is actually when the American Indian Movement was first born, because we think that the American Indian Movement is not only an advocate for Indian people, it is the spiritual rebirth of our nation. (*Akwesasne Notes* 1974:60)

Is the American Indian Movement leading the spiritual rebirth of American Indians? Or was the investigating Congressional Subcommittee correct to conclude, in September 1976, that "the American Indian Movement does not speak for the American Indians. . . . It is a frankly revolutionary organization which is committed to violence" (quoted in Vizenor 1984:135)? What about the "tribal people who will continue to revise the vain advertisements of peripatetic mouth warriors [shooting off at the mouth] as statements of traditional visions" (Vizenor 1984:138)?

Late in February 1973, Wounded Knee Creek once again became the site of a momentous event in United States Indian history. Both events at Wounded Knee were armed confrontations between American Indians and United States forces. Both events were lavishly reported in the popular media across the United States, and both became symbols of the cruel oppression of the First Americans by the raw power of the United States government. Contrary to the popular notion, the Wounded Knee Massacre in 1890 was only tenuously connected to the Ghost Dance religion and had little, if any, effect on it. Was the 1973 siege of Wounded Knee part of the agonizing contractions giving rebirth to American Indian spirituality, or was it the joint creation of egotistical renegades and headline-hunting reporters together preying on a gullible, romantic public?

Wounded Knee, in 1973, was a maddening mix of lofty rhetoric and dirty politics, dirty rhetoric and lofty vision. In 1973, it was chic to be radical; it was frustrating to be American Indian; it was the turning point in the Vietnam War, a year when marches and bombings seemed to have forced the United States government to respond to the uncompromising demands of militant protesters. The siege at Wounded Knee was a happening very much of its time. Comparing it and its leaders with the events and leaders of 1890 shows how extraordinarily complex "Indian affairs" have become in the century since the end of the Indian Wars.

BACKGROUND HISTORY

The people whom the United States Census counts as American Indian are identified as descendants of those living in North America prior to the European invasions of the sixteenth and later centuries. Several hundred nations, each with its distinct language and customs, occupied the continent, and there were additional hundreds of smaller, less formally organized societies in the less productive regions. The native peoples had no common name for the inhabitants of the continent, no common culture. Europeans labeled them "American Indians" and looked for common denominators to simplify dealing with them. From time to time, Indian nations allied to fight European encroachment: The League of the Iroquois may have developed in part as a response to the European threat. The 1680 Revolt of the Pueblos in the Southwest and the 1675 "King Philip's War" in New England, Pontiac's War of 1763, and Tecumseh's of 1811 are other well-known examples. The Indian nations remained autonomous until they were subordinated by the colonizing European and then the United States governments. Then they were organized by the United States government into administrative units that in many instances only loosely correlated with native residential or political groupings. Thus a continent of hundreds of independent nations was overrun by an immigrant nation classifying its native adversaries under a single racial term, "American Indian," and eventually designating "tribes" as much for administrative convenience as native social validity.

More than a century of living under United States governance taught "American Indians" that numbers bring clout. Fragmented into scattered "tribes" isolated on reservations or lost in the masses of cities, American Indians could be ignored by lawmakers and bureaucrats. The Ghost Dance religion had reinforced Indian peoples' conviction of the worth of their heritages, but its focus on religious affirmation was not an effective mechanism to bring about political alliance and action. Indians had created intertribal organizations designed to lobby for Indian rights as early as 1911, when the medical doctors Charles Eastman (Dakota Sioux) and Carlos Montezuma (Yavapai), anthropologist Arthur Parkman (Seneca Iroquois), attorney

Thomas Sloan (Omaha), Episcopalian minister Sherman Coolidge (Arapaho), and musician and writer Zitkala-sa [Gertrude] Bonnin (Lakota Sioux) formed the Society of American Indians. These were Indians determined to use political opportunities as other highly educated Americans did, to work for the betterment of their constituency, the Indians.

The Society of American Indians lasted only a dozen years. Its brief existence revealed the obstacles to an effective national advocacy group of Indians. Leaders at ease in upper-class urban American society where power lies lost touch with Indian communities. Indian communities had no means of selecting representatives to national voluntary organizations such as the Society, or of regularly communicating their problems and ideas to the national leaders. Diversity of backgrounds, both of ancestral cultural traditions and of contemporary education and professions, separated members of the Society and induced clashes between them. They could agree, with Dr. Eastman, that American Indians had "fallen into the clutches of a Bureau [of Indian Affairs] Machine, which controls our property, our money, our children and our personal rights" (quoted in Iverson 1982:148). The question was how to extricate their peoples from the strangling "Machine."

In 1924, American Indians were at last recognized as American citizens, by an Act of Congress. Many states nevertheless continued to refuse Indians the right to vote—two states denied that right to Indians until 1948—and citizenship did not free Indians from the paternalistic control of the "Bureau Machine." The generation of Indian leaders who had formed the Society of American Indians in 1911 aged and were eclipsed by Euro-American reformers espousing the Indians' cause. Chief among them was John Collier, who began working in settlement houses in poor neighborhoods in New York City and moved on to champion the Pueblos he met hobnobbing with the artists gathered around the heiress Mabel Dodge and her Taos Pueblo husband, Tony Luhan. In 1933, President Franklin Roosevelt appointed Collier Commissioner of Indian Affairs. Indians were to participate in Roosevelt's New Deal—through the Bureau Machine.

In 1934, Collier created an Indian Reorganization Act designed to bring American democracy and, through it, economic improvements to the Indians. Reservations were to be divided into electoral districts, residents were to elect by secret ballot representatives from their districts, the representatives were to meet in a Tribal Council and enact reservation business and rules just as other Americans in municipalities and counties did. Collier prepared a model constitution for tribes to consider and adopt. All over the United States, Indians were lectured on this wonderful democratic government and urged to vote for one on their reservation. The only flaw in Collier's vision of revolutionary democracies for Indians was that it did not allow for democracy: As paternalistic as his predecessors, Collier handed down *his* plan and badgered the recipients to endorse it. Grumbling and rumbling coursed through the land, but not too loud (or was it that the Machine couldn't hear well?). Indians, like everyone else, were gripped by the Great Depression, and ideals like democracy took a back seat to federal programs promising employment or relief. Civilian Conservation Corps (CCC) and Works Progress Administration (WPA) projects sometimes brought greater prosperity to a reservation than it had achieved in the 1920s.

World War II abruptly terminated Collier's programs, though the apparatus of district-based elected Tribal Councils ruling through tribal constitutions remained. Thousands of Indians were recruited into the armed forces, and thousands more were recruited to move to cities to work in industries. Most of the Indian soldiers saw themselves defending their homeland, even though it had long been subjugated by foreigners, and fought enthusiastically. (Back home, their families revived the rituals invoking success in war.) Indian war workers enjoyed the good pay and camaraderie on the "Home Front." When the war ended, many families stayed in the cities, and some veterans joined them. Los Angeles, San Francisco, Seattle, Minneapolis, and Chicago became home to thousands of Indian families.

Seeing these Indians apparently assimilated into urban populations, the government declared such assimilation its goal. Were Indians delighted at this prospect of escaping the clutches of the Bureau Machine? Strangely, no. Wartime industries welcomed every able-bodied comer, and racial discrimination was muted by the "war effort." A different picture greeted emigrants from the reservations in the 1950s. The Relocation Policy dumped Indians into competition for jobs, poor housing, and prejudice in the cities. Poverty on the reservations was numbing but not so bitter. Resentment built against the government for its relocation campaigns and flared when the government announced plans to terminate the special status of reservations judged capable of supporting their residents without government assistance. Indians wanted out of the clutches of the Bureau Machine, but they did not want to be assimilated willy-nilly into the mass of the populace and to lose their heritages of nationhood.

In 1944, the National Congress of American Indians had been organized as a "United Nations of the tribes," more consciously seeking to actually represent the diversity of Indians, though using the government's list of tribes as an organizational base. After a decade of Tribal Councils, younger, formally educated Indians felt comfortable with the official designations of tribes, arbitrary though many of them were. In 1960, Indian college students organized the National Indian Youth Council. The next year, anthropologists at the University of Chicago engineered an American Indian Chicago Conference of 450 Indian delegates from 90 tribes. The National Congress of American Indians cooperated in the Chicago Conference. All the meetings called for an end to paternalism and for the "freedom from bondage" that Charles Eastman had demanded back in 1918, but at the same time they called for the right to continue their Indian communities as they themselves determined, that is, self-determination.

What had these college-educated Indian leaders achieved by the end of the 1960s? Termination of reservations and relocation of Indians to cities were no longer government policy goals. After almost a century of non-Indian Commissioners, the Bureau of Indian Affairs was again headed by an Indian (an Iroquois like his predecessor Ely Parker, who was Commissioner in 1869).

President Lyndon Johnson specifically included the Indians in his War on Poverty, with a National Council on Indian Opportunity chaired by the Vice-President, and the Civil Rights Act was extended to American Indians in 1968. Johnson said he wanted to stress Indian self-determination.

"INDIANS OF ALL TRIBES"

Alcatraz Island in San Francisco Bay had been a notorious prison. The prison was closed and the island declared "excess property" by the federal government in 1964. Some Sioux living in the San Francisco area crossed to the island and filed a claim on the "excess property," but their claim, though pressed to the United States District Court, was not taken seriously. Five years later, November 1969, San Francisco area Indians were upset when the San Francisco American Indian Center, a community center for thousands of Bay Area Indians, burned down. A few Indians crossed over to Alcatraz again and, with news media observing, once more announced a claim to the still-empty island. They were promptly evicted by U.S. marshals. A couple of weeks later, on November 20, several boatloads of Indians, mostly college students, landed on Alcatraz determined—*self*-determined—to either convert the abandoned facilities to Indian community use or force wider awareness of the needs and aspirations of that community.

Supported by older people on the mainland, the young Indians organized themselves as "Indians of All Tribes" and formed a cooperative settlement that hung on for nineteen months. The young men and women, and a few children, enjoyed adopting items of "Indian dress" (some movie stereotypes, some more authentic), informal evening powwows of Indian music and dancing, and a general exploration of what might be called Indian values and culture. This was not quite the same process as that stimulated on the early reservations by Jack Wilson's creed. The Alcatraz community encompassed Indians from dozens of tribes, many of them unable to speak their ancestral languages and unfamiliar with much of their peoples' traditional religions. Revival of suppressed beliefs and practices, unlike in 1890, awaited learning those beliefs and practices. (This was not entirely a matter of the students' having lived in cities and spent so much time in Euro-American schools. Indian communities tended to assume that young people were not yet ready for serious religious instruction and that they would apply themselves to such learning as they settled into middle age.) The task was complicated by the diversity of peoples represented on Alcatraz.

"Indian" was a European construct. The category was laid upon the hundreds of nations across the continent when the European invasions began. Over four hundred years of usage had strengthened the term, and a century of government administration of "American Indians" had reinforced it. The college students on Alcatraz were accustomed to thinking of themselves as "Indian" as well as "Oglala" or "Mohawk" (or, somewhat generically, "Sioux" or "Iroquois"). Most important, they, like the founders of the Society

of American Indians, knew that insistence on native diversity would weaken
their efforts to deal with the dominant society that smothered that diversity.

Meanwhile, in Minnesota other young Indians actively worked to forge a
national Indian crusade. As Dennis Banks recounted the story (Zimmerman
1976:118–128), it all began when he was in prison for parole violation, in
1967–1968. He read about civil rights marches, about protests against the
Vietnam War, and about treaties between Indians and the United States.
Where were Indians in the protest actions? In 1968, when he was back in
Minneapolis, where he had worked in community social programs in the early
1960s, Banks organized a meeting of members of a number of local Indian
groups. Police harassment of Indians was the topic; the men formed an American Indian Movement Indian Patrol to cruise the streets of the section of
Minneapolis where Indians congregated, watching for incidents of harassment. Recruiting a fellow Chippewa (Anishinaabe in their own language),
Clyde Bellecourt, to assist, Banks pushed to extend the AIM beyond Minneapolis, beyond Minnesota. Ironically, Banks was employed at the time by
the Honeywell Corporation to bring more Indian employees into the company, an affirmative-action gesture, and initially Honeywell benignly granted
Banks a leave of absence to build AIM. A powwow later in 1968 in Minneapolis brought in new associates, Russell Means, an Oglala working in
Cleveland, Herb Powless, a Wisconsin Menominee living in Milwaukee, and
Clyde's brother Vernon, who would start an AIM chapter in Denver.

By late 1969, when the Bay Area Indian students landed on Alcatraz,
AIM had a national structure of chapters in cities with substantial Indian
populations. Its leaders were constructing an ideology affirming an Indian
identity supported by an Indian religion, which turned out to be basically
Oglala Lakota, thanks to the handy paperback *Black Elk Speaks* and the
willingness of several Oglala *wicaša wakan* to assist neophytes. Leonard Crow
Dog, from Rosebud Reservation, became active in AIM, and Frank Fools
Crow, from Pine Ridge, welcomed AIM members as he did others seeking
spiritual guidance and blessing in the Oglala manner.

Here the story gets sticky. While Frank Fools Crow, born in about 1890,
is respected as a legitimate traditional Oglala leader who saw a responsibility
to intercede when events involving his people called for godly (that is, *wakan*)
wisdom, Leonard Crow Dog and other AIM organizers have been viewed as
ambitious politicians. Their claims for a spiritual foundation to AIM, for AIM
as a religious as well as a political movement, have met skepticism. Dennis
Banks, Russell Means, and others have been criticized as "born-again Indians," men who saw the light of adulation and dollar bills attending them if
they wore their hair in braids and donned beads. AIM has been accused of
trying to coopt the Alcatraz occupation and the "fish-ins" protesting interference with treaty-stipulated Indian fishing rights in Washington state. Can
AIM be a religious movement if it chooses confrontational tactics? Can it be
a genuine Indian movement if its leaders have lived so long in cities, once
dressed in middle-class business style, and may lack fluency in their ancestral
Indian language?

AIM leaders argued that their organization could succeed because it got away from the genteel elitism of the Society of American Indians and its successor educated-Indian groups. AIM muscled in, literally. AIM could succeed, they argued, because its concerns went beyond local problems; it had learned from the genteel groups the necessity of raising pan-Indian issues. AIM sought a universalistic Indian religion to legitimatize its pan-Indian ambitions. Its leaders were consciously creating, or cobbling together, a movement new but not alien to American Indians, a late-twentieth-century kind of Ghost Dance, they insisted. In fact, Leonard Crow Dog actually revived the 1890 Ghost Dance ritual to express AIM's purpose.

The year 1972 was marked by a grand media event, the Trail of Broken Treaties. Spurred partly by the fish-ins, eight Indian organizations began marching from Seattle to Washington, D.C., to present their demands to the President. AIM made itself prominent on the march. Press and television photographers attracted by the colorful costumes worn by some of the marchers gave media coverage to the project, particularly when at last it reached Washington at the end of October. The Indians expected to meet with high government officials at the Bureau of Indian Affairs (BIA) headquarters, but were rebuffed. While representatives from the march were talking with lesser officials, other marchers grew restless—it is rumored that government informers who had infiltrated the Trail assembly egged them on. Security guards ordered the Indians to leave the BIA building, but the Indians were angry and barricaded themselves in the building. They held out for six days, until three of President Nixon's top negotiators offered them promises of serious consideration of their demands and no prosecution of charges stemming from the takeover of a government building. The Indians cleared out, their way sweetened with thousands of dollars to pay their expenses back to their homes. Behind them, Broken Treaties marchers left trashed offices; with them, they took cartons of documents they believed would substantiate their claims that the federal government had not only reneged on treaty promises, but had colluded with private corporations to let non-Indian businesses reap vast profits from Indian resources.

The Trail of Broken Treaties came to be remembered as the Trail of Trashed Offices. However justified the Indians' frustration, vandalism in the BIA building only deepened the public stereotype of American Indians as savages, while the protesters' readiness to depart once negotiators had obtained cash for their return confirmed other Indians' suspicions that greed for money played a part in the affair. Had Russell Means been honest when he insisted, "We are trying to bring about some meaningful change for the Indian community. . . . We didn't come here to grab hold of a building. We came here to work. The situation looks very positive because the negotiators realize our commitment here—that we are willing to die" (quoted in Weyler 1982:50)?

Was that easy rhetoric or was Russell Means speaking as a true Oglala? At the beginning of this century, a young Lakota man, Mato Sica ("Bad Bear"), had explained to James Walker, an earnestly concerned physician, on Pine Ridge:

Every able-bodied boy was taught that he should become a warrior, not only in order to defend himself and his people against hostile persons, but to get honor by doing something against an enemy which required cunning and bravery. When one had accomplished such things, he was entitled to certain decorations and privileges, and he could compose songs in honor of himself which the women would sing, and the more renowned he was the more often would the women sing his songs. A warrior was entitled to a seat among the councilors, and his influence in the council was in proportion to his renown as a warrior. (Walker 1982:27)

Perhaps the century-long war the Lakota fought against Euro-American invaders had enhanced warriors' prominence in Lakota society, but there can be no question that Mato Sica expressed sentiments common among Lakota at the end of the nineteenth century. Nick Black Elk and his elderly friends harped on their war experiences as they talked with John Neihardt; earlier in the reservation period, the talented Lakota artist Amos Bad Heart Bull depicted battle scenes far more than any other topic, though he was personally disinclined to fight. Being prepared to go to war was the mark of an honorable Lakota man.

PRELUDE TO THE SECOND WOUNDED KNEE

Means soon had another opportunity to declare, "All we want is justice, and our demands are just. If our demands are not met, we will die here" (quoted in Jorgensen 1978:36). Pine Ridge Reservation was deeply troubled. It was (and is) one of the poorest districts in the entire United States. Its prairie is too dry for any large-scale agriculture other than ranching, which could not support the growing population on the reservation. Remote from cities, railroads, and major highways, the district cannot attract industry or build service employment. Without jobs, some Oglala hung around bars in the small towns on the periphery of the reservation in Nebraska and South Dakota. Prejudice against Indians ran rampant in many of these towns, themselves economically straitened.

Raymond Yellow Thunder was a middle-aged alcoholic Oglala who accepted drinks from a pair of Euro-American young men, brothers, just outside the reservation one day in 1972. As the three became more and more drunk, the young men started abusing Yellow Thunder. Gross and cruel, their "fun" went on for hours until they had beaten their victim to death. The brothers were arraigned on charges of manslaughter, not murder, in a state court and sentenced to only a year in jail.

Wesley Bad Heart Bull quarreled with a Euro-American man in a bar near the reservation in January 1973. The next day, the man stabbed Wesley to death. Again, the murderer was arraigned on manslaughter charges, and this time there was not even the excuse that, as with Yellow Thunder, it was a drunken binge. Wesley was a young man. His mother was angered by the cavalier attitude of the local police to this murder of an Indian. She asked for support from the man who had been pressuring South Dakota officials to redress apparently racially discriminatory hiring on federally financed projects. He in turn invited Dennis Banks to look into the situation. A meeting was set up for February 3–5, 1973 in Rapid City to discuss the issues targeted by the Oglala Sioux Civil Rights Organization, formed the previous year by Pine Ridge people. After the meeting, a car caravan of Indians drove to the county seat where the Bad Heart Bull case was heard. County officials refused to let all the riders in the caravan into the courthouse. Police tried to evict them, and they fought back. The result was the arrest of thirty-four Indian protesters, among them Mrs. Bad Heart Bull. The outraged, grieving mother was sent to prison on riot charges, and her son's murderer was acquitted of manslaughter!

On Pine Ridge Reservation, hundreds of residents were convinced that Tribal Chairman Richard Wilson, elected in accordance with John Collier's Indian Reorganization Act, was corruptly using tribal monies to enrich himself and his friends. The suspicious residents formed the Inter-District Council of the Oglala Sioux Tribe, which sought to impeach Wilson. Wilson saw AIM's hand in the action against him, as well as in the melee at the Custer, South Dakota, courthouse, which had exacerbated, he felt, troubles between his people and the Euro-Americans he wanted to cooperate with. Wilson banned AIM from Pine Ridge.

On February 26, 1973, several of the older Pine Ridge district chiefs met with members of the Oglala Civil Rights Organization. They decided to invite AIM, through Russell Means, to come to Pine Ridge to assist in dislodging Wilson. Clyde Bellecourt was already in South Dakota, at Leonard Crow Dog's home on neighboring Rosebud Reservation, where he had attended a memorial service for Nick Black Elk on February 23. Dennis Banks was on Cheyenne River Sioux Reservation, in northern South Dakota, discussing grievances with residents there. He drove down to Pine Ridge, with several other cars of Cheyenne River Sioux people.

On the evening of February 27, 1973, the arriving visitors joined the Oglala district chiefs and the other Pine Ridge people eating dinner in the Calico community hall on Pine Ridge. Dennis Banks recalled:

> These two women, Helen [Ellen] Moves Camp and Gladys Bissonette, got up. Gladys spoke for about twenty minutes in Lakota. . . . Then she turned around to us and she spoke to us in English. She started crying, and she said to us that we had to realize that for many years the Oglala Sioux had lost their will to fight. "For many years," she said, "we have not fought any kind of battle, and we have forgotten how to fight." Then she asked if we would help them.
>
> Then Helen Moves Camp got up and she spoke along the same lines, and she started to cry during her talk to me. She came right up to me, crying, and she was begging for help. She said that if it's the last thing we do, we should fight for Indian people, and fight there. (quoted in Zimmerman 1976:125–126)

Mrs. Moves Camp and Mrs. Bissonette not only spoke in terms of nineteenth-century Lakota values, but they used traditional Lakota formal oratorical discourse, including crying as a sign of sincerity in their pleas. (Men as well

Figure 30. The graveyard at the hamlet of Wounded Knee, in 1987.

as women cry in this oratorical mode; pleading for spiritual aid is called *hanbleceya*, "crying for a vision.")

Ellen Moves Camp remembered that the district chiefs at the Calico community hall recommended, "Go ahead and do it, go to Wounded Knee. You can't get in the BIA office and the tribal office, so take your brothers from the American Indian Movement and go to Wounded Knee and make your stand there. Throw them off and don't announce that you're going to Wounded Knee. Say you're going to Porcupine for a meeting" (quoted in *Akwesasne Notes* 1974:31).

A caravan of several dozen cars and pickups formed and drove toward Porcupine. First they passed through the agency town of Pine Ridge, where they glimpsed armed U.S. marshals called to the reservation by Richard Wilson, who anticipated trouble. The caravan reached the tiny hamlet of Wounded Knee, between the towns of Pine Ridge and Porcupine. Oglala had never forgotten the massacre of Big Foot's band in 1890. Americans, including Oglala, had been reminded recently of the event through Dee Brown's 1971 best-selling *Bury My Heart at Wounded Knee*, and many Oglalas had been irritated when the non-Indian owners of the Wounded Knee Trading Post had tried to capitalize on the book's popularity with roadside billboards advertising the "Massacre Site." There had even been an effort to bring tourists to a Sun Dance ceremony to be held near the Trading Post.

The caravan stopped before the mass grave and monument to the 1890 victims, and Frank Fools Crow, Pete Catches, another respected Oglala *wicaša wakan*, and Leonard Crow Dog led the prayers at the gravesite. According to the AIM members there, Crow Dog then said:

Here we come going the other way. It's just like those Indian soldiers in Big Foot's band who were going to Pine Ridge, and now they're coming back. We're those soldiers, we're those Indian people, we're them, we're back, and we can't go any further. Wounded Knee is a place where we can't go any further. (quoted in Zimmerman 1976:127)

Dennis Banks said later:

We all knew when he got done talking that . . . we would have to do or die at Wounded Knee. . . . Everything pointed to one course of action—retake Wounded Knee, seize it, hold it, and let the chips fall. . . . The medicine men [*wicaša wakan*] brought wisdom to us. They gave us the spiritual direction we needed. . . . There was no going to Porcupine, there was no writing letters to the government and sending them demands any more. That's exactly what the medicine men said to us—"when you put your words on paper, then they step on them." So the direction that we received was good. (quoted in Zimmerman 1976:127–128)

By late February of 1973, Pine Ridge Oglala had watched on television ten years of protests over denial of rights to black Americans. They had watched five years of protests over the war in Vietnam against Indochinese. They had protested the murders of their own Oglala by neighbors who got off with lighter sentences than a petty thief. They resented Richard Wilson's high-handed ways, abetted, they were sure, by the BIA, the Bureau Machine. They had endured another bitter South Dakota winter in drafty little houses crowded with men and women who could find no jobs, see no future. The Oglala were joined by Russell Means' AIM friends, looking for a crusade to follow the Trail of Broken Treaties. With Dee Brown's catchy title, months on the best-seller lists, ringing in everyone's ears, AIM seized its opportunity.

THE SECOND WOUNDED KNEE

Committed now to a do-or-die stand at Wounded Knee (the Second Wounded Knee), people from the caravan went into the hamlet. They explained to the owners (who were non-Indian) of the Wounded Knee Trading Post that they were staging a protest and took some weapons and ammunition from the store. The eleven residents of the hamlet were not alarmed. Around them, the protesters settled in, deploying a few young men with guns around the perimeter of the hamlet. Beyond it, the FBI and U.S. marshals, already on Pine Ridge for two weeks at Wilson's request, set up roadblocks and battle stations. Wounded Knee was under siege.

Later the same evening, an employee of the U.S. Department of Justice who had been in the hamlet approached the marshals to deliver to the federal government the "Demands" of the Oglala Sioux Civil Rights Organization:

—for a hearing, under Senator William Fullbright [as they spelled his name], on treaties;
—for an investigation, under Senator Edward Kennedy, of the Bureau of Indian Affairs in all its offices;

—for an investigation, under Senator James Abourezk of South Dakota, into the South Dakota reservations.

The "Demands" concluded,

The only two options open to the United States of America are: 1. They wipe out the old people, women, children, and men, by shooting and attacking us. 2. They negotiate our demands. (*Akwesasne Notes* 1974:35)

Senators Abourezk and McGovern, the two senators from South Dakota, along with aides of Senators Kennedy and Mansfield, met with a deputation from the occupiers of Wounded Knee at one of the government roadblocks on March 1. By then it was clear that none of the hamlet residents, at first assumed to be held as hostages, was being forcibly detained. The senators and aides listened to the deputation's list of grievances and promised to do what they could to meet the "Demands." Meanwhile, the siege of Wounded Knee continued.

Both sides, Indian and government, received reinforcements. Armored vehicles were brought in to support the FBI and marshals. Indians from Pine Ridge and from other reservations and tribes, reporters, church representatives, and a few political radicals walked over the prairie hills to sneak between roadblocks into the hamlet. Marshals and Indians each dug in, excavating bunkers to shoot from. Gunfire was exchanged from time to time, each side insisting the other had fired first. Within the hamlet, people set up community kitchens, assigned sleeping spaces, and scheduled guard shifts and religious rituals. By March 8, the Indians counted 167 men, women, and children inside their ring of bunkers. That day, the younger men had their faces painted with red ocher earth paint in the nineteenth-century Lakota manner to signify they were ready to fight and die for their nation.

Orders from the government were to keep the news media away from Wounded Knee. With the AIM leaders together in this remote settlement, the government saw its opportunity to wipe out the rebels' movement. AIM contacted the media through runners slipping out and returning as guides bringing in reporters and television cameras between the roadblocks. Press photographs showed big beefy marshals and armored combat vehicles outside the village, and slender young Indian men, some of them recently returned from service in Vietnam, crouched down with rifles protecting their women. Thousands of rounds of ammunition poured into the picturesque hamlet with its white frame Catholic church and meandering Trading Post, and reporters let the American public know of the attacks.

The siege of Wounded Knee lasted for seventy-one days. The National Council of Churches got a negotiator into the village; black civil rights activist and minister Ralph Abernathy went in. On March 10, a Saturday, the roadblocks were lifted to encourage Indians to peacefully abandon their position, but instead of leaving, they welcomed new supporters. Several of the Oglala traditional chiefs, men descended from nineteenth-century band leaders who had been ritually invested as district and ceremonial leaders, met in a tipi set up close to the 1890 mass grave. Out of their discussion came, on March 11, a Declaration that the Oglala were now the Independent Oglala Nation: "[T]he Oglala Sioux people will revive the Treaty of 1868. . . . [W]e are a sovereign nation by the Treaty of 1868. We intend to send a delegation to the United Nations . . . [and] abolish the Tribal Government under the Indian Reorganization Act. Wounded Knee will be a corporate state under the Independent Oglala Nation" (*Akwesasne Notes* 1974:55). To seal this proclamation, the besieged new nation marched, led by Chief Frank Fools Crow, from the tipi to the 1890 mass grave, linking the last Oglalas to have grown up in the truly independent Oglala nation to their descendants and friends in the new Independent Oglala Nation.

Back and forth through March and April the negotiations went on between the Independent Oglala Nation and the United States government. Food ran low in Wounded Knee and had to be backpacked in at night, a difficult way to supply some two hundred people. Soup made from instant mashed potatoes flavored with popcorn seasoning was the only meal on some days. Daily community meetings coordinated the various task groups—kitchen, clinic, security, communications, negotiations—and discussed plans. Anyone and everyone was encouraged to speak, informally, and decisions were arrived at by consensus rather than vote. Evenings, non-Oglala were ceremoniously inducted as naturalized citizens of the Independent Oglala Nation. The community felt uplifted by a strong spirit of brotherhood.

On March 22, the same day that Leonard Crow Dog led a Ghost Dance ritual, a Legal Defense Committee was formally organized in Wounded Knee. The Indians wanted to negotiate directly with White House aides, the Senate Foreign Relations Committee (the Independent Oglala Nation being a foreign nation), or top staff of the Department of the Interior (within which was the Bureau of Indian Affairs). The basis for negotiations was to be the 1868 treaty between the United States and the Oglala nation. The United States government refused, insisting that the issue was political insurrection expressed through burglary (goods taken from the Wounded Knee Trading Post), disorderly conduct, inciting to riot, and conspiracy. Assistant attorneys general were sent from the Department of Justice to deal with these crimes and civil disobedience.

In 1973, Americans were watching film clips from the Vietnam War on the daily news shows. Now they saw an American hamlet, right in South Dakota, attacked with round after round of bullets. They saw the wide blackened strips from the grass fires set by government agents around the hamlet. They saw people stopped at the roadblocks and frisked, their cars searched as uniformed men held guns on them, people threatened with being taken to jail in handcuffs for driving along a South Dakota road. The parallels with Vietnam were horrifying.

On April 5, an agreement was signed by both sides, in the presence of reporters, that the government in Washington would host traditional tribal chiefs to develop a Presidential Treaty Commission to examine the 1868 treaty. Alleged misconduct of Richard Wilson and other members of the

Tribal Council would be investigated and, if confirmed, prosecuted. The siege would be lifted and the besieged, disarmed. That meant the Indians would surrender all their weapons to the fully armed United States troops. Living as they were beside the mass grave of Big Foot's band, the Indians could not consent to such a replay of that 1890 morning. They had to insist on mutual and simultaneous disarmament. The government in 1973, like that in 1890, wanted to keep machine guns trained on the Indian camp while 180 U.S. marshals with pistols made a sweep, planned for seven o'clock in the morning of April 7. Said the head marshal, "We just want to neutralize and sanitize the area" (*Akwesasne Notes* 1974:150).

Leonard Crow Dog suggested an alternative plan, one he had seen, he said, in a vision: Government agents and their tanks should pull back, and as they did so, the warriors of the Independent Oglala Nation, to show their good faith, would stack their weapons in the tipi near the 1890 grave site. They would place a peace pipe in front of the tipi to ensure that no one would touch the weapons inside. A government negotiator replied, "We can do a much better job protecting you folks in the village if we stay in our present" armed positions (*Akwesasne Notes* 1974:152). The negotiations continued, with a cease-fire.

On April 17, at dawn, three small planes flown by non-Indian members of anti-war protest groups dropped large sacks of food over Wounded Knee. Marshals on the hills ringing the village saw the sacks drop but could not know their contents. Apparently, they assumed the bags held weapons and began a barrage of the hamlet that, for the first time, took a life, that of Frank Clearwater, who said he was Apache and with his pregnant wife had hiked into Wounded Knee just the day before to offer what help he could. Clearwater had been sleeping in the Catholic church when he was shot. He was taken to a hospital in Rapid City, South Dakota. His wife left Wounded Knee to go with him, but was arrested and held in jail for several days. Richard Wilson refused to allow Frank Clearwater to be buried on Pine Ridge Reservation because he was not Oglala (at that, an Oglala woman commented, "I guess we'll have to dig up all them white ranchers then" [*Akwesasne Notes* 1974:222]). Eventually, Clearwater was interred on Leonard Crow Dog's land on Rosebud Reservation.

Another fire fight occurred on April 26 and 27. Buddy Lamont, an Oglala who had survived a tour of duty in Vietnam, was shot in front of one of the Wounded Knee bunkers on April 27. He was a native of Pine Ridge, and his death angered his many relatives on the reservation. On May 1, the Lamont family worked to prepare the traditional funeral feast for Mrs. Lamont's only son while negotiations resumed between the government and the Independent Oglala Nation. Several other Indian men had been wounded in the barrages of April 27, and a U.S. marshal had been seriously wounded in late March.

The negotiators met in a pair of school buses parked between the government's encircling forces and the hamlet. One bus was supposed to be for discussion of "military" questions, that is, disarmament, and the other was for "political" questions, the 1868 treaty and the allegations against Richard

Wilson and his Tribal Council. Despite the unrealistic separation of "military" from "political" issues, an agreement was at last created, spurred by a letter from White House Special Counsel Leonard Garment promising a meeting between White House aides and the Oglala traditional chiefs later in May. The chiefs signed the agreement on May 5, and the next day Buddy Lamont's funeral was held in Wounded Knee.

After the funeral, many of the people in Wounded Knee left. Those who did not, including the original residents of the hamlet, were taken out on May 8 to be searched, fingerprinted, and photographed. While they were away, men from the Department of Justice Community Relations Service (*not* the hated U.S. marshals who maintained the siege) went through the village and took all the weapons they found. These "victors" pulled down the AIM flag flying from the church steeple and raised the United States flag to the accompaniment of a speech and gun salute.

AFTERMATH OF WOUNDED KNEE 1973

Wounded Knee 1890 and Wounded Knee 1973 had similar outcomes: The general American public far away from the reservation expressed sympathy for the Indians and outrage at what seemed a show of force out of proportion to the actual threat, then quickly forgot the stale news. Nothing much changed for the Indians. Richard Wilson claimed a win over Russell Means, by 200 votes, in a tribal election held February 7, 1974. Means filed a complaint of irregular voting with the U.S. Commission on Civil Rights, which in October 1974 returned its report confirming many irregularities and sloppy procedures during the election. Nevertheless, Wilson retained the office.

Russell Means and Dennis Banks went on trial in Minneapolis on a series of federal charges brought against them as principal leaders of the seizure of Wounded Knee. Dozens of other members of the occupation were tried separately, on lesser charges, in a different court. After months of testimony and argument, the Minneapolis judge found such misconduct on the part of the FBI and Department of Justice agents that the charges against Means and Banks could not be sustained. Nevertheless, harassment of AIM leaders continued. Leonard Crow Dog was jailed for his participation in an incident with government agents in Wounded Knee, paroled, then jailed again for "aiding and abetting assault" when he and relatives threw a couple of rowdies off the family property on Rosebud Reservation. His home was raided in 1975 by a large party of FBI agents looking for evidence in the murder of two agents on Pine Ridge (not Rosebud) Reservation three months earlier. That murder has never been solved. Violence escalated on the reservation. Some months later, the body of a young AIM adherent, Anna Mae Aquash, was discovered rotting beside a stream on Pine Ridge, a bullet in her brain. Aquash, a mother, was a Micmac Indian from Nova Scotia, Canada, who had come to Wounded Knee in 1973, had married there, and stayed on, working for AIM goals. Aquash's murder also has never been solved.

Traditional Oglala leaders did meet with White House aides in Washington in September 1975. President Gerald Ford stopped in and shook hands with the chief of the Sioux delegation, Frank Fools Crow. On September 5, 1975, Fools Crow, at the invitation of Senator Abourezk, gave the prayer opening that session of the United States Senate, the first *wicaša wakan* to do so. Richard Wilson lost the chairmanship of the Oglala Tribal Council in an election monitored by the Federal Mediation and Conciliation Service. The Council struggled with the severe economic problems besetting Pine Ridge and adjacent Rosebud Reservations, and by 1982 had developed a two-pronged attack: creating local landowners' cooperatives to feed the communities and try to produce surplus to sell to Denver and other markets, and demanding expansion of Oglala lands.

The Oglala Tribe filed claims in court for that part of the 1868 Great Sioux Reservation lying in the Black Hills west of Pine Ridge Reservation. The Black Hills are still prime hunting grounds, and Lakota traditionally sought spiritual guidance and blessing on their high buttes. The Black Hills also are believed to hold highly valuable uranium and other mineral resources, and much of the Oglala claim is leased to major corporations for mineral exploration. The State of South Dakota earns substantial tourist dollars from parks it operates in the Black Hills. Privately owned tourist businesses, ranchers, loggers, and the U.S. Forest Service are additional vested interests in the claim lands. All of them oppose the Oglala suit.

On April 4, 1981, a caravan of cars left Pine Ridge Reservation to camp in the disputed Black Hills, on U.S. Forest Service territory. Russell Means, his brother Bill Means, and other AIM members were in the group. They argued for exclusive use of 800 acres of the territory, not only on the basis of the 1868 treaty, but also because the 1978 American Indian Freedom of Religion Act, Public Law 95-341, says that "it shall be the policy of the United States to protect and preserve for American Indians their inherent right . . . to . . . exercise the traditional religions . . . including but not limited to access to sites, use and possession of sacred objects, and the freedom to worship through ceremonials and traditional rites." About fifty men, women, and children formed the camp, named Camp Yellow Thunder in memory of Raymond Yellow Thunder, the Oglala murdered in 1972. Tipis were the shelters, campfires the means of cooking. Children were to be schooled in traditional culture, providing a third ground for the land claim: Under a federal law dating from 1897, schools or churches can be built on government-owned forest lands. With children being educated and a sweatlodge purifying participants in the frequent rituals, Camp Yellow Thunder was both school and church. Leonard Crow Dog played his accustomed role as spiritual leader.

Camp Yellow Thunder was touted as an exercise in the Oglalas' claim to the "sacred" Black Hills. Many Oglalas, including a tribal attorney, took strong exception to the action of occupying the 800 acres in the Hills. They thought the argument that the 1978 American Indian Freedom of Religion Act justified the occupation might be a red herring confusing the Oglala Tribe's claim based on the 1868 treaty. The Tribe desperately wanted the land for an economic base: land for hunting, land with water for agriculture, land in a popular vacation area where the Tribe could earn cash through developing tasteful resorts (as, for example, the Mescalero Apache do on their reservation). That the Hills had been a favorite location for spiritual vision quests was only a small part of the Tribe's need and irrelevant to its insistence that the United States fulfill its obligations stipulated in the treaty.

A decade after the Second Wounded Knee, reporters for the *Denver Post* found that families on Pine Ridge Reservation had the lowest income of *all* American families. Unemployment hit 82 percent on the reservation: More than five-sixths of people seeking employment could find nothing. On the entire reservation, covering three million acres and home to 13,300 Oglala in 1984, only 2300 jobs were listed, and 1600 of these were funded by the government. Pine Ridge tried to attract industry and ended up with two small plants, one assembling fish lures and one making moccasins.

Agricultural development, severely limited at best by the aridity of most of the reservation, is stymied by two political-economic conditions as well, fragmentation of holdings and lack of capital. Fragmentation is the result of the 1887 Dawes Allotment Act, by which Congress decreed that each Indian family be allotted one quarter-section (160 acres) of land for a subsistence farm. No stipulation was made in the law that the allotment be adjusted according to the agricultural potential of the land; on the Plains, one whole section, 640 acres, is considered the bare minimum for a working farm. Once each family on a reservation had its allotment, the "surplus" land was to be opened for sale to non-Indians. No effort seems to have been made to give Indians the best land on their reservations, so that much of the acreage most suited to agriculture ended up outside the adjusted reservations. Nor was land set aside in anticipation of Indian population growth. Each generation since the allotment, which was conducted on Pine Ridge in 1906, divided up the meager family acreage among its children.

Lack of capital for development stems from the trust status of reservation lands, which, even though allotted, usually remained under the administration of the Bureau of Indian Affairs. An Indian generally could not put up his allotment as collateral for a bank loan because it was encumbered by being part of the reservation; therefore, Indians could not raise capital as non-Indian farmers expect to do. At first, after 1906, Pine Ridge Oglala slowly built up cattle herds by ignoring, in effect, the allotments and running the cattle as on an open range. World War I brought high prices for beef, and Indians were encouraged to sell a large proportion of their stock, while non-Indian ranchers surrounding the reservation pressed to lease Indian land to expand their own ranges. The agent in charge of Pine Ridge after the war did not oppose the practice of leasing, so the attraction of gaining an income without working persuaded many Oglala to abandon their own ranching efforts. In the 1920s, agriculture on the western Plains became more capital-intensive, with a continuing trend to larger acreages, specialized heavy machinery, expensive irrigation, and supplementary feeding of cattle. Handicapped in obtaining loans, Indians resigned themselves to letting the non-

Indian ranchers and wheat farmers pay them the low fees that were all they could get for the "unimproved" land. John Collier in the 1930s, and the Oglala Tribe in recent years, promoted the formation of cooperatives to pool allotments and funds, but these seem to run into dead ends: World War II labor and agricultural market demands disrupted the New Deal cooperatives, and the 1970s idea of the Tribe providing low-cost loans to Oglala to buy out other heirs, in order to consolidate allotment holdings for development, began to exhaust tribal funds. Half a million dollars would be required, it was estimated, to minimally fund a community agricultural cooperative, even if no money were required to obtain land. At bottom, the Oglalas' problem has been that they tried to pull themselves up by their bootstraps but discovered they didn't have any bootstraps.

That frustration—the experience of hopes dashed again and again for lack of resources, legal entanglements, or the effects of world markets—breeds anger and factionalism. Reservations were deliberately located in areas remote from cities and transportation networks in order to protect Indians from being readily victimized by unscrupulous Euro-Americans. (Remote areas were less desirable for Euro-American colonization, and that made it easier for officials genuinely concerned about Indian vulnerability to get support for these locations from others unconcerned about Indian welfare.) Indians have been for the most part rural people, suffering with other rural Americans the onslaught of agribusiness and franchises that severely reduced the viability of family farms and businesses. When Indians move to cities, they, like many other rural Americans, encounter prejudice in hiring and housing, which in the case of Indians is exaggerated by racism. Cost of living in cities is so high that even with a full-time job, a person may be near the poverty level, so the hope of many Indians that city employment will provide means to assist relatives on the reservation is seldom fulfilled, and the Indians may move back to the reservation where at least there are family, friends, and clean air.

On the reservation, frustration continues, and hostility builds between advocates of doing this, advocates of doing that, and cynics advocating doing nothing. Pine Ridge Reservation seethed with such factionalism in 1972, one bloc agreeing with Richard Wilson's efforts to cooperate eagerly with non-Indians, another bloc urging adamant pursuit of the 1868 claim to the Great Sioux Reservation lands, and cynics reminding everyone of the white man's record of double-dealing and treachery.

The Second Wounded Knee can be interpreted as an outburst of frustration, the tip of the iceberg of resentment felt by Indians after a century of subordination. The wonder is only that there have not been more such incidents. Wounded Knee 1973 can be interpreted, as the government has wanted to, as the machinations of a violent, rebellious bevy of radicals tied to Communist Cuba, the Palestine Liberation Organization, the Irish Republican Army, and the Black Panthers. Wounded Knee 1973 can be interpreted as a local disagreement between Pine Ridge factions, blown out of proportion by news media looking for colorful copy. And Wounded Knee

1973 can be interpreted as the AIM leaders want to, a resurgence of American Indians devoted to their ancestral beliefs and way of life.

All the above interpretations are true. Wounded Knee 1973 was economic and political frustration boiling over, it was in keeping with the spirit of the times of radical protests, it was a real hope of sparking an Indian renaissance. At Wounded Knee in March 1973, an AIM spokesman tried to explain the event in Lakota terms:

> The American Indian Movement sees itself as a new warrior society for Indian people. There is a varying concept of warrior society. To white persons, the warrior is the armed forces. It's the guy that goes out there and fights and kills for his people. But Indian people have never had hired killers. Warrior society to them means the men and women of the nation who have dedicated themselves to give everything that they have to the people. A warrior should be the first one to go hungry or the last one to eat. He should be the first one to give away his moccasins and the last one to get new ones. That type of feeling among Indian people is what a warrior society is all about. He is ready to defend his family in time of war—to hold off any enemy, and is perfectly willing to sacrifice himself to the good of his tribe and his people. That's what a warrior society is to Indian people, and that's what we envision ourselves as, what we idealistically try to be. I'm not saying that we are all completely selfless or any kind of saints. But we try, with the spiritual direction of our holy men, to get ourselves to the point where we don't have the avarice and greed that is so much a part of Anglo—of white—society in the United States.
>
> We believe that the power of this universe is held within our peace pipe. It is a pipe of peace, a pipe that at all costs tries to guide us in avoiding any deaths by our own hands, any violence on the part of the American Indian Movement. And if anyone will check back into the history of the American Indian Movement, though we take a very strong stand for our people, we've never killed anyone. We have never had violence unless violence was perpetrated on us first.
>
> The real violence in America is committed by the Government against our people. The real violence is the fact that on a reservation our women are taken and raped in the back seat of these police cars. The real violence is that our children are never able to learn to live in a society that is completely alien to them, and so they suffer tremendous disorientation in their own lives which many times leads to suicide, or drunkenness—which is another form of suicide—or drugs. The real violence is when the Bureau of Indian Affairs, who is supposedly holding our lands in trust for us—because they say we are incompetent to handle our own affairs—reduces our land base by 160 thousand acres or so every year. (quoted in *Akwesasne Notes* 1974:61–62)

During the 1960s, the real violence in American society blazed on television screens every evening on the news. Not only Indians were repelled. Throughout America and Europe, too, citizens wanted a calmer life, to smell the flowers and see blue sky. Thousands congregated on the California hills and the meadows of upstate New York, letting their hair grow, throwing off their clothes, smoking pot, listening to folk singers and the Beatles. Hundreds went to Indian reservations seeking nature's children, the supposed "primal

mind" of "primal people" in touch with Mother Earth. (It is rather discom-
fiting to be Indian and have a stranger look upon you as a "primal person"!)
Black Elk Speaks blossomed in the jeans pockets of these pilgrims. Some of
the pilgrims from an urban life were of Indian ancestry, perhaps from marriage
between a Euro-American and an Indian, perhaps with both parents Indian
but from different tribes, having met in off-reservation schools. Some of the
pilgrims got involved in AIM or Camp Yellow Thunder or another Indian
protest, and some of the leaders of these protests manipulated the naiveté of
the pilgrims.

Out of the 1960s came also a quite different movement, self-determination
demanded by subjugated peoples around the world. George Manuel, a Shus-
wap Indian from British Columbia, Canada, led this movement of "indigenous
peoples" whom he terms the "Fourth World." (The major Western and Soviet
bloc nations constitute the First and Second World; the "less-developed"
nations are the Third World; the Fourth World comprises those nations no
longer recognized as such, existing entirely within dominant nations as "internal colonies." The Oglala Nation is a Fourth World nation existing as an
internal colony of the United States.)

Manuel organized a World Council of Indigenous Peoples in 1975, and
won recognition of it as an NGO (Non-Governmental Organization) by the
United Nations, to which it has submitted briefs describing the adverse conditions oppressing many of its members, from Australian Aborigines to Northwestern European Sami ("Lapps") and many Indian peoples of North and
South America. In 1982, thousands of delegates and spectators convened in
Regina, Saskatchewan, for a World Assembly of First Nations tying together
the World Council of Indigenous Peoples and the Canadian Indian "First
Nations," which were pressuring the Canadian government for much more
autonomy for its Indian bands, that is, for self-determination. Along with
panel discussions and workshops, the Assembly set up a tipi camp housing
"Elders" to whom people could repair for spiritual counseling. This camp,
the Assembly declared, was its "heart."

Wounded Knee 1973 was not a scene from a "primal world" of uncor-
rupted spirituality, but it did endeavor to proclaim the values of communal
goals and generosity. Lakota tradition did not permit authoritarian rule, of
which Richard Wilson was accused, or wealth accumulated at the expense of
others in the community and withheld from them. Sharing, government by
consensus, respect for all life, human and animal, and for the world we are
given are values widely espoused by a majority of American Indians, by
Americans concerned with ecological protection, by members of the Green
political parties in Europe, and by "bioregionalists" endorsing a political
structure based on ecologies rather than on military power. The Indians at
Wounded Knee, like the young "Indians of All Tribes" on Alcatraz, like the
World Council of Indigenous Peoples, like Nick Black Elk and Jack Wilson,
wanted Indian self-determination, not in a narrow egotistical sense but as the
persistence of Indian communities with their own cultures. Wounded Knee
1973 demanded recognition of Indians' inalienable rights to life, liberty, and

the pursuit of happiness given by "the Laws of Nature and of Nature's God," according to Thomas Jefferson. The framework of the event was its era of protests against war, the armaments race, and despoliation of the environment. The roots of the event were deep in the history of the continent invaded by millions of Europeans bent on colonizing. The catalyst was the bitter antagonism between Richard Wilson's Tribal Council and many of the traditional district chiefs. Wounded Knee 1973 accomplished none of its aims. In the longer view, it demonstrated that the "first nations" of our continent remain very much alive. Jack Wilson's vision, Black Elk's vision—Frank Fools Crow's vision—hold true in the midst of what a tourist sees as grinding poverty. How long it will take to overcome the "clutches of the Bureau Machine" and the reservations' intractable economic handicaps cannot yet be guessed.

Figure 31. "AIM Is Cool," sprayed on pillar, Wounded Knee, 1987.

PART TWO | Social Science Perspectives

PART TWO | Social Science Perspectives

PART TWO | Social Science Perspectives

7/Prophet Dances

Nineteenth-century anthropologists were pioneers, using methodology from natural history and their own intuition to work out topics and approaches fruitful in the study of American Indians. The general shift, at the turn of the century, from such "democratic" science—its practice open to anyone regardless of formal education or training—to the modern demand for professional credentials applied to anthropology. Advanced academic training became a prerequisite for anthropological investigations and encouraged more rigorous research. This and the following two chapters look at a series of anthropological analyses of Jack Wilson's Ghost Dance and similar cases—as they become in social science—of American Indian events.

Social science is an invention of modern culture. Many American Indians today resent their peoples having been used as objects of analysis. They feel they have been treated as less than human. The complaint is justified, but it is more than a matter of racist stereotypes parading as scientific findings. The dehumanizing "objective science" approach to the management of human beings has been applied to factory and office workers, soldiers, students, and even babies. The many instances of an excess of objectivity, which ignores the emotions, highlight the difficulty of understanding human behavior. If we abstract too much, we are likely to overlook relevant factors, and if we try to encompass everything that occurred, we cannot see the forest for the bewildering number of trees. The best anthropologists have tried to strike a balance between "thick" and "thin" description, to use a phrase made famous by the contemporary American anthropologist Clifford Geertz. The three chapters here go back over the material "thickly" presented in Part One, to show how social scientists have tried to understand the events.

It was forty years after Mooney's 1896 report before another major anthropological study addressed Jack Wilson's Ghost Dance. The new study was more narrowly ethnohistorical or, as it was put then, "culture-historical." It represents the kind of unemotional, meticulous archival and ethnographic research that is described, not always in admiration, as scholarly. Its author, Leslie Spier, was one of the younger members of the first generation of Ph.D. anthropologists. Like Margaret Mead, another of his generation, Leslie Spier was trained at New York's Columbia University by the exacting Franz Boas. The story of the conflict between the Smithsonian's Bureau of American

Ethnology and Columbia's Boas sets the stage for twentieth-century studies of the Ghost Dance and similar American Indian events.

Franz Boas, a German Jewish immigrant, led the effort at the turn of the century to establish anthropology as a field of study within universities. Boas was appalled at some of what passed for anthropology at the time, particularly the racist slurs claiming to be based on scientific evidence. Boas' conceptualization of anthropology had been strongly influenced by a dramatic year he had spent living with Inuit ("Eskimos") on Baffin Island in the Canadian Arctic. He had conceived the project as deductive social science, hypothesizing that the Inuit, inhabiting some of the most extreme climatic conditions endured by humans, would have a culture entirely shaped by the exigencies of survival. He found that, contrary to his hypothesis, they enjoyed a wealth of songs, poetry, stories, myths, and jokes as they relaxed in their *iglus* (houses), superbly engineered for the climate. Boas realized there was nothing "primitive" about his Inuit companions; they exhibited intelligence, sensitivity, and rationality comparable to these qualities in Europeans.

His experiences living with Inuit strengthened Boas not only to refute claims that American Indians are "primitive," but also to emphasize the value of inductive procedure, of collecting an abundance of data before venturing a hypothesis. (Boas was a highly knowledgeable statistician, which contributed to his predilection to demand an abundance of instances.) When Boas became a professor of anthropology at Columbia, he impressed upon his students the crucial importance of collecting adequate data. An anthropologist must begin with "participant observation," talking with the people studied, observing and taking notes on their everyday and ceremonial behavior and on their manufactures. Field study will stimulate questions, some to be explored in discussion with informants in the field; some to be researched in archives of historical documents, government censuses, and policy papers; and some to be followed up in collaboration with botanists, zoologists, metallurgists, and other scientists. Boas was very critical of the nineteenth-century anthropologists who constructed grand theories of human cultural evolution without leaving their comfortable libraries.

At the Bureau of American Ethnology (BAE), the anthropologists for the most part resented Boas' steadily increasing influence over the young science of anthropology in America. Their research was generally similar to that of Boas and his students, and they saw no reason to take a back seat to "Professor" or "Doctor" So-and-So from Big University. Boas tended to use a classroom tactic of showing his students the errors in selected published works in anthropology, without balancing these by pointing out good examples of research other than his own. This made him appear arrogant. His efforts to obtain jobs for his graduates at the BAE as well as in universities were interpreted as ambition to dominate the practice of anthropology throughout America. Boas seemed to personify the elitist German model of science remote from ordinary citizens' participation and control.

Exacerbating, and confusing, the conflict between the nineteenth-century Smithsonian's ideal of democratic science and the modern insistence on professionalism was an ugly racism, a revival of the Know-Nothing politics that in the mid-nineteenth century had tried to exclude immigrants from citizenship. The revival around 1920 sought scientific data to prove the inferiority of all peoples other than Protestants from northwestern Europe (that is, "WASPs"—white Anglo-Saxon Protestants). It is interesting to note that in 1919 James Mooney was the only BAE anthropologist who did not censure Franz Boas for "unpatriotic" sentiments. Mooney's Irish Catholic origin made him, almost as much as Boas, a target for WASP racists. Mooney, like Boas, rejected the grand evolutionary theories that called the Indians savages of inferior capacities. Mooney was indefatigable in collecting data firsthand, and his field experiences continually reinforced his conviction that Indians should enjoy the same freedoms of assembly, opinion, and religion as other Americans.

James Mooney died in 1921. During the decade of the 1920s, American anthropology completed its shift from the democratic science of its first half-century centered in the Smithsonian's BAE, to its contemporary university-dominated form. To a considerable degree, American anthropology incorporates structures and principles advocated by Boas and his Ph.D. students, the most important of which is the insistence that racist denigrations of non-European peoples fail to find sound scientific support. In recent decades there has also been renewed appreciation of the solid worth of much of the research of nineteenth-century pioneers such as Lewis Henry Morgan, a lawyer by profession, and John Wesley Powell, the founder of the BAE; that both of these men accepted theories of "racial" progress conventional in their time does not diminish the value of the primary data they innovatively recognized, collected, and organized, nor of their unstinting efforts to promote anthropology. Twentieth-century anthropology takes the nineteenth-century wealth of observations and the Boasian critiques to reconstruct, as seen in this chapter, the broader context of Jack Wilson's religion, and, as described in the next two chapters, to venture a series of explanatory models.

Leslie Spier took a position teaching at the University of Washington in Seattle in 1920, immediately after completing his Ph.D. with Boas. Thoroughly rehearsed in the skills of anthropological methodology, he began field researches with Indians of the Northwest. He noticed mentions of round dances during which people would fall into a trance and then rise up and prophesy. Carefully collating these descriptions with similar items from the journals and memoirs of explorers and missionaries, Spier found this form of religious ritual common in the Pacific Northwest and the adjacent intermontane Columbia plateau (Washington, Oregon, Idaho, and western Montana). The region included the range of the Northern Paiute, of which the Tövusi-dökadö formed a band. Was Jack Wilson's Ghost Dance perhaps a traditional round dance?

From his meticulous researches, Spier concluded that what he termed the "Prophet Dance," the community round dance about a leader during which trances, exhortations, and prophesying usually occurred, was a pre-European ceremony to which elements of Christian ritual had been added during the nineteenth century. The Christian elements could have come in part from an emigration of Catholic Iroquois Indians, originally from near Montreal, Quebec, who settled among the Flathead in western Montana about 1820, and in part from the teachings of Spokan Garry, a chief's son of the Spokane people who was sent to school in Manitoba and returned about 1830 fluent in English and familiar with Protestant Christianity. Spier felt that Jack Wilson's religion was basically a version of this "Prophet Dance" known to the Northern Paiute, and the incorporation of elements of Christianity was already a generation-old tradition when Wovoka was born.

Much of Spier's conclusion had been anticipated in James Mooney's chapters, in *The Ghost Dance Religion*, on the Smohalla and Indian Shaker churches of the Pacific Northwest. Mooney had pointed out the similarities between these religions and Jack Wilson's, and indicated Wilson's opportunities for contact with their practitioners. What Spier added was a narrative, rich in historical and ethnographic detail, of early-nineteenth-century religious movements in the Northwest; what he excluded, but Mooney had not, were comparisons beyond the target region of North America. Spier's monograph on the "Prophet Dance of the Northwest" is an example of the careful, tightly focused comparative study, drawn from well-documented ethnohistorical data, that anthropologists preferred in the twentieth century.

After the publication of Spier's work in 1935, anthropologists debated both the antiquity he claimed and the apparently Christian elements in the "Prophet Dance." Deward Walker (1969) was able to redirect the discussion by bringing in new archaeological and ethnohistorical data delineating the eighteenth century as the "protohistoric" period of increasing importation of European goods via Indian entrepreneurs. These Indian entrepreneurs were not only those who had traditionally traded along the Columbia River Valley from the Pacific into the Rockies, but, beginning in the 1790s, were also eastern Indians—Iroquois and Abenaki—traveling as trappers and traders and, by 1799, settling a colony near Edmonton, Alberta.

Among desired items of European origin were horses, which, traded up from the south, became common in the Northwest after 1730. Horses facilitated the accumulation of goods by carrying much greater loads, when camps were moved, than people or their former pack animals, dogs, had been able to. The market for horses among Indian peoples stimulated raiding, both for horses and for human captives who could be exchanged as slaves for horses from Spanish colonists in the American Southwest. Captives sometimes escaped and managed to return to their own people, bringing with them knowledge of foreign ways.

By the 1780s, contacts between Indian communities were so frequent that a smallpox epidemic could spread rapidly throughout the northern Plains and Northwest. One-third or more of the people in many Indian camps and villages died in the epidemic, suddenly depriving the survivors of their loved ones' knowledge and skills. Deward Walker believes that this tragic disruption of communities, added to the greater awareness of foreign peoples resulting from the increase in trade, stimulated the emergence of the religious movement that appeared in early-nineteenth-century historical records consulted by Spier.

Christopher Miller (1985) agrees with Walker that the protohistoric period in the Northwest incorporated such radical changes—in population reduction, in the frequency and volume of intersocietal trade, and in hunting and material accumulation patterns adapted to the use of horses—that new religious understanding had to be forged. Miller, in accordance with a recent trend in anthropology to study European and Euro-American along with non-European cultures, balanced his research in Northwest Indian beliefs and history with an account of the Protestant missionary efforts there beginning in the 1830s. The Indians supposedly were awaiting the coming of a man with a book, from which he would teach wisdom, and of course this expectation made them welcome Christian explorers and missionaries carrying books. The prophecy about the man with a book was recorded fifty years after it was allegedly made and three decades or more after men with books began traversing the Northwest, and the reliability of the dating and content of the prophecy is open to question. Miller's study does strengthen Walker's contention that the end of the eighteenth century, the protohistoric period, was likely a time of considerable shifts and innovations in Northwest Indian societies. How much of the Indian cultures recorded by the first explorers in the early nineteenth century represented survival of ancient traditions, and how much innovation, is uncertain.

Ethnohistorian Melburn Thurman (1984) uncovered another innovator, an Ojibwa woman—whose name has been forgotten—who came to live in about 1813 with the Kutenai in western Montana. This woman's homeland was the American Midwest, and she lived there when the Shawnee prophet Tenskwatawa flourished. Tenskwatawa had experienced a vision in 1805: The Master of Life had instructed him to repudiate all things European and preach to all Indians a return to their own way of life. The prophet's brother, Tecumseh, assisted him in spreading the word, and by 1811 they had forged a military alliance of the Indians in the eastern Midwest that was ready to drive out the invaders. The alliance was defeated that year in the Battle of Tippecanoe (Ohio).

Was the nameless Ojibwa woman involved with the Shawnee prophet, or perhaps with other Indian prophets appearing at least since 1762 with similar messages to the Indians desperately holding the American frontier at the Appalachians? Whatever her origin, the woman appeared to the Kutenai and their neighbors to be a charismatic person, with qualities of both woman and man, gifted with spiritual knowledge and power. She traveled along the Columbia River, preaching and prophesying, and also went north, reaching the Chipewyans in northern Canada in 1813. Thurman suggests she may have introduced the ritual of dancing, trance, and prophesying to the Northwest, finding ready acceptance in this era of change.

Quite a different perspective is given by the ethnographer Robin Ridington, who has lived with the Beaver (Sekani) Indians in northern British Columbia, Canada. The Beaver live by hunting, trapping, and fishing in the forest. Like the Paiute far to the south, the Beaver depended, in the days before rifles, on surrounding groups of animals and driving them to slaughter by waiting armed men. Like the Paiute, the Beaver surrounds were managed by persons who had experienced spirit-sent visions of successful surrounds. In 1799, Beaver visited a fur trade post, probably their first contact with Europeans. The trader recorded that the group was led by a man named Makenunatane, called the Swan Chief because he was a visionary whose soul could fly like a swan high up into the heavens. Makenunatane was famed for producing highly successful game surrounds and was reputed to be the most generally knowledgeable person with whom his people were acquainted.

The Beaver told Ridington that Makenunatane had introduced Christian practices to them, explaining that these practices were a "shortcut to heaven" revealed to him in his visions. Ridington interprets this to mean that Makenunatane realized that his people would be shifting from communal game surrounds to more individualized hunting for the fur trade and that the rituals of the traders, that is, Christian practices, would be appropriate in their coming trade-oriented life. His habit of keen observation furnished the Swan Chief with perceptions that crystallized in prophetic visions similar to those that had always guided the Beaver.

A point that Ridington (1982) emphasizes is that the Beaver, in common with other Indians hunting in the Canadian forests, consider technology to consist in the *knowledge* of how to carry out operations, rather than in the tools used: They carry their technology in their heads, more than in toolboxes. They therefore did not easily distinguish between European traders' Christian rituals and the means by which Europeans obtained the goods to trade (indeed, without speaking English or traveling to eastern cities, how could the Beaver correctly figure out how European goods came to be available?). From this perspective, the Swan Chief was instructing his people in practical means to get trade goods, as he instructed them at other times in the means to obtain meat. Northwest Indians' eagerness to take up Christian practices may have been, from this perspective, motivated by materialistic wishes as well as religious enthusiasm.

Precedents for Jack Wilson's and the *wodziwob* Fish Lake Joe's "Prophet Dance" seem abundant in the Northwest, although we cannot determine whether the ritual form was truly aboriginal or was an innovation in the protohistoric period. Comparing the Northwest with the Northeast, where the protohistoric period began about A.D. 1500 and the fully historic soon after 1600, two similarities appear. In the Northeast, Indians experienced a series of religious movements, which, in the case of Dekanawidah's founding of the League of the Iroquois, may or may not be related to European incursions—the evidence pro and con the League's being "purely" aboriginal is much debated. The second similarity lies in the Protestant evangelical missions that, as Miller realized, must be considered together with any discussion of historic Indian religions.

In the early 1740s, the American colonies engaged in a Great Awakening preached by George Whitefield, an English evangelist who introduced revival meetings to America. Both in the 1740s and in the Second Great Awakening in the eastern United States in the early nineteenth century, participants in the revival meetings often fell into frenzied dancing, trances, and vision experiences recounted in prophesying. In England, converts fired up by Whitefield's associates John and Charles Wesley exhibited similar "enthusiasms." The American First Great Awakening inspired a Narragansett Indian, Samuel Niles, to take over a Narragansett Indian Christian congregation. Niles was illiterate but familiar with the Bible, and preached in the "enthusiast" manner popularized by Whitefield. William Simmons, the anthropologist who has studied the Narragansett Indian Church, notes (1983) that "enthusiast" preaching was not so different from the agitated praying and exhortations of the traditional Narragansett *powwow* ("doctor or spiritual healer," equivalent to the Lakota *wicaša wakan*). Further, the revival preacher as well as the traditional *powwow* frequently claimed to heal the sick.

Both Protestant Americans and North American Indians include many who value spiritual leaders who combine fervent exhortations to a "clean, honest life" with claims to healing power. In both cultural traditions, the role has been embodied in a long series of preacher-healers—including today several famous television evangelists. It is possible that the American Indians learned the role from the Europeans they observed, but the probability seems to be that there were, from the first, parallels between native religious behavior and many Christian evangelists. A few Christian missionaries, such as the French Jesuit Gabriel Druillettes who worked with Abenaki Indians in Maine beginning in 1646, tried to emphasize steady prayer and quiet nurturing of the sick in contrast to the *powwows'* excitation, but even Father Druillettes could be goaded into dramatic ritual, as when he offered Mass with fervent beseeching of God to relieve the hunger of his traveling party. (And it worked. The Abenaki killed three moose right after Mass.)

Some of the parallels between Christian and American Indian religious behavior go deep into human physiology. Building up rhythm and loudness of speech from slow and soft to fast and loud tends to catch listeners up, their own heartbeats increasing in rapidity along with the speech rhythm to produce a feeling of excitement. (There are anthropological studies documenting this, for example, Rybak 1977.) Gestures may focus listeners' attention on the speaker to the point where the audience is almost hypnotized. Changing the pitch of voice, now high, now deep, induces subconscious mood changes in listeners. Frenzied dancing tends to induce hyperventilation and cause that mental dissociation we term trance. These basic human physiological responses are likely to have been independently discovered in many societies and also to have facilitated borrowings of rituals from culture to culture. Thus human physiology makes it probable that societies will discover and institutionalize "enthusiast" behavior. The tendency for humans to find such behavior fulfilling and valuable leads to the entanglement of tradition and borrowings we have seen in the history of "prophet dances."

The "Prophet Dance" was a popular ritual among Indians of the American Northwest throughout the nineteenth century. Leslie Spier was correct in confirming James Mooney's insight that Jack Wilson's travels to the north probably contributed to his blessing of the round dance with trance and prophesying as the proper expression of worship. To what degree Iroquois emigrants and the Ojibwa woman introduced Indian revivalism and Christian symbols in the Northwest we shall never be sure. What we see clearly from Mooney's wide-ranging comparisons, and from all the historical investigations into possible antecedents of the Ghost Dance ritual, is "a hope and longing common to all humanity," as Mooney phrased it, manifested through behavior rooted in human physiology and common experience.

The long record of "prophet dances" and the striking similarities between them and the dancing, trances, and prophesying of Protestant evangelist revivals point to a likelihood that religious movements promoting such expression have not only a long history, but a long future. Black Elk and his scribes John Neihardt and Joseph Brown stressed visual images, but contemporary American Indians continue also the physical enactment of rituals. So do Pentecostals, a growing segment of American Christians. Though Leonard Crow Dog's revival of a Lakota version of Jack Wilson's Ghost Dance ritual did not catch fire, one can see simple round dances in community and worship groups all over America. Trances and inspired prophesying are regular occurrences in many churches as well as among still practicing traditional Indians in the Northwest. The physical form of Jack Wilson's religion was not original, nor is it extinct.

8/Deprivation and the Ghost Dance

Not all Indian peoples took up the Ghost Dance around 1890. Why did some reject the call to dance into renewal of an Indian world?

Mooney visited Navajo, on their huge reservation in northern Arizona and adjacent New Mexico, during the winter of 1892–1893, and inquired about the Ghost Dance. Three years earlier, in the winter of 1889–1890, Paiutes had come to the Navajo to proselytize Jack Wilson's religion, but none of the Navajo with whom Mooney spoke credited the Paiute evangelists with any success. Dr. Washington Matthews, a physician with the Navajo who was among the first to record their language and beliefs, and A. M. Stephen, a Scotsman who lived with the Hopi nearby for years and also learned to speak Navajo, confirmed Mooney's information that the Navajo had not been interested in Jack Wilson's religion. Stephen wrote to Mooney that he had asked Navajo friends, over a campfire, about the "messiah"; *datsaigi yelti*, said Stephen's Navajo companions, "it is worthless talk."

Dr. Matthews suggested to Mooney that the Navajo were relatively rich, with well over a million sheep and goats and over a hundred thousand horses for a tribal population officially counted as 16,000 persons in 1892. Comfortably off, most Navajo had no reason to want the present world destroyed. Stephen, living in another section of the reservation, wrote Mooney that his Navajo friends had heard that a mythical personage was returning, accompanied by the Navajo dead, to cast out non-Indians and force Pueblo neighbors, the Hopi and Zuni, to stay close to their own villages, out of Navajo territory. The Navajo would then again enjoy the extensive lands once theirs. Most Navajo scoffed at this "rumor," as Stephen termed it. It may be that they felt they did not need any mythical spirit to give them back their land, because the United States government had already doubled their original reservation, giving them parcels of hundreds of thousands of acres in 1878, 1880, 1882, and 1884. (More large parcels would be added in the twentieth century.) The Navajo—in arid country of no interest then to Euro-American homesteaders or miners—were thus in a situation quite opposite to that of the Lakota around 1890.

To see the Navajo as well off in 1890 ignores several significant conditions. As much as one-third of the Navajo at this time did not own sufficient livestock for a livelihood. While this one-third, of course, included children, the aged, and disabled persons who would inevitably be dependent upon others, it also included able-bodied adults who had lost the few animals initially provided by the government when it released the tribe in 1868 from their four-year imprisonment in a concentration camp. Navajo customarily give sheep and goats to children as soon as they are able to herd them, to help the children develop responsibility and good work habits, so the one-third of the population without resources would not have simply been the young, the aged, and the disabled—many children would have been stock owners.

Navajo who did not own enough livestock to support themselves might live with better-off relatives, but that burden might force the relatives to the edge of want. Government rations remained an important part of the Navajo economy, as did manufacture of jewelry and rugs. A Navajo mother sitting outside her hogan home weaving a rug looks picturesque; from the point of view of an economic analysis, she is a laborer whose production may earn a substantial portion of her family's income. When the international market for wool was glutted and prices were low, wool was turned into rugs by the Navajo weavers, their input of labor resulting in a slightly higher return on the wool of their herds than if they had sold the raw wool directly for low prices. When the wool market prices were higher, more Navajo wool was sold raw and fewer rugs were woven.

The market for rugs, bought by Euro-Americans for home decoration, was quite different from the market for raw wool, so regardless of the price of wool, Euro-American traders selling rugs made on the reservation tried to maintain rug manufacture by directly employing weavers, providing them with wool, and instructing them to use the patterns most popular with the

Figure 32. Navajo family carding, spinning, and weaving (blanket and belt) beside their home. Photographed by James Mooney in 1893.

buying public. Rug weaving was a cottage industry integrated into the United States economy, not an ancient Navajo custom. Jewelry was similarly manufactured and merchandised. Men and women without substantial herds supported themselves in these industries.

Comparing the Navajo with the Lakota and with the Tövusi-dökadö in 1890, both Navajo and Paiutes had been integrated into a viable regional economy, while the Lakota had been cut out by the loss of so much of the Great Sioux Reservation. Dr. Matthews had served in Dakota Territory before his assignment to Navajo country, so when he answered Mooney's inquiry in 1891, he could not but be struck by the difference between the Navajo and the Lakota he had known, more recently at war, suffering a sudden complete loss of the animals they depended upon, and drastically robbed of their land. Compared with the Lakota, the Navajo could be termed rich. Compared with the Tövusi-dökadö, still able to hunt and gather wild food staples to supplement their regular wage employment on farms, a substantial minority of the Navajo were not so well off. Why did the Navajo scoff at the Paiute proselytizers of Jack Wilson's religion?

A series of sociologists tried to determine whether acceptance of the Ghost Dance was associated with recent loss of bison herds, or perhaps with another factor. The Navajo, after all, had never depended upon bison as Plains Indians had. Michael Carroll (1975) counted, from Mooney's monograph, those tribes "exposed to the Ghost Dance" and then the tribes that had been bison hunters, and through statistical formulae tested whether these were largely the same peoples. Carroll was skeptical, adding another test of correlations between societies with "unilineal kin groups" and those without. ("Unilineal kin groups" are groups of persons organized by descent through their fathers— "*patri*lineal"—or through their mothers—"*matri*lineal." These "patrilineages" or "matrilineages" usually own land and other property, extending user rights to their members. They may also be responsible for policing their members.) Carroll hypothesized that societies with "unilineal kin groups" gave members stronger social support, and this would make them less anxious, less prone to religious cult proselytizing. Carroll concluded from his statistical tests of correlations that his hypothesis was likely to be true, that few (but still, some) tribes described as being organized in patrilineages or matrilineages took up Ghost Dancing. The correlation between loss of bison hunting and Ghost Dancing was not so close. Navajo social organization includes matrilineages, so Carroll could conclude that his hypothesis explained why the Navajo never took up the Ghost Dance.

Several sociologists responded to Carroll's paper. Most of them criticized Carroll's categorizing of tribes. Some of the tribes listed as having lost bison hunting had lost it many years previously, and some in the 1880s, but Carroll had lumped all of them together. Another criticism asked how certain he could be that a tribe listed by Mooney as not participating in Ghost Dancing was "exposed to"—knew about—the religion. For the Navajo, Mooney describes considerable proselytizing and direct evidence of rejection, but he lacked time to visit numerous communities that did not participate.

Some tribes had already been converted to a comparable alternative religion. Wananikwe, a Dakota woman, in 1876 developed and proselytized throughout the upper Midwest a religion quite similar to Jack Wilson's. Followers of her Dream Dance religion were uninterested in the Ghost Dance. If one wants to figure out why the Lakota did, and the Navajo did not, take up the Ghost Dance, questioning should be restricted to those other peoples who similarly had been proselytized, and perhaps to those who had no comparable religion already. One of Carroll's critics pointed to the Dream Dance adherents to claim that tribes whose land had been allotted, by government order, into individual family farms by 1889 had been too broken up to form any congregation. This critic apparently did not know that in spite of allotment of their lands, these tribes already had espoused a similar religious doctrine with a congregational ritual promoting social solidarity.

The most ambitious of the sociologists using statistics to discover possibly significant correlations is a Cherokee, Russell Thornton (1981, 1986). He took seriously the idea that Ghost Dancing would bring back souls. Would conversion to the Ghost Dance correlate with heavy population losses? That is, did tribes suffering severe population loss seek to rebuild through the Ghost Dance ritual? Thornton compared tribe populations in 1870, 1890, and 1910, and concluded that there was a statistical tendency for the tribes that had lost the greatest number of people between 1870 and 1890 to take up the Ghost Dance. Further, he argued that taking up the Ghost Dance around 1890 had really worked, that those tribes had stemmed their population losses—not, obviously, by bringing back the dead, but by encouraging the living to remain in what appeared to be a newly viable community.

Thornton's correlations are so full of exceptions requiring special explanations that they are, in the end, weak. Major criticism of his efforts rests upon his basic data, which are weaker even than the correlations and expose the difficulty of explaining historical events by quantitative material factors. Population figures for American Indian peoples are more estimates than solid data. Indians were not counted in regular U.S. censuses until 1910, and the basis for counting someone as an Indian is personal self-identification. Between one census and another, an individual can change his or her identification. Tribal populations are actually counts of persons legally enrolled in a government administrative unit called the tribe, which can include people of mixed ancestry and exclude "full bloods" who for one reason or another happen not to be legally enrolled. Reservation populations represent another, and different, government administrative unit, in many instances lumping together members of separate ethnic groups who were assigned to the same reservation by government officials. Thornton's population figures represent too many arbitrary units, and too many estimates rather than firm counts, to be satisfactory data for his statistics.

From Carroll to Thornton, efforts to tease out the "cause" of the Ghost Dance religion's acceptance from simple statistics have proved flawed. Though the Navajo can be held up as supporting any of the correlations proposed relating Ghost Dancing to loss of bison, or social solidarity, or population, those who know the people and their history have not agreed that these correlations are significant. Two such anthropologists have accepted the challenge of explaining Navajo rejection of Jack Wilson's religion.

David Aberle suggested "relative deprivation" is a condition precipitating religious movements. Aberle defined "relative deprivation" as "a negative discrepancy between legitimate expectation and actuality" (Aberle 1962:209). British anthropologist Peter Worsley, in a study of recent religious movements among Melanesian (South Pacific) native societies, anticipated Aberle by pointing out that what is legitimate expectation to a Melanesian, according to Melanesian customs, may be fantasy to a European brought up with a different understanding of personal rights in property. Thus, "legitimate expectation" must be understood in the local society's terms. "Relative deprivation," too, is local: The Melanesians, like the Beaver Indians in 1799, felt deprived of imported objects once they had visited trading posts, in spite of continued availability of their traditional goods.

Deprivation was an obvious explanation for Navajo social movements in the 1930s. By the mid-1930s, the number of livestock grazing the Navajo Reservation threatened to destroy the quality of the range. A related threat came from engineers building Hoover (then called Boulder) Dam on the Colorado River, intended to supply water to southern California. The engineers predicted that overgrazing in the Colorado Basin would precipitate erosion that would silt up Lake Mead, the reservoir behind the dam. They called the Navajo Reservation "Public Enemy No. 1 . . . causing the Colorado Silt Problem" (quoted in White 1983:251).

The Bureau of Indian Affairs decided to reduce the size of Navajo herds,

Figure 33. Navajo shepherd beside his hogan home, early 1900s.

"improve" their quality (that is, replace local stock with more marketable animals of standard breeds), and get more Navajo into farming instead of stock raising. Some 400,000 animals were purchased by the government from Navajo owners, but not in the same proportion from all herds. Indian families with large herds were saddened by the loss of some stock, while families with only a few animals saw their livelihood wiped out. Subsistence farming had always included livestock, with animals substituting for crops in bad crop years, and vice versa. Navajo families forced to sell most of their small herds could not survive by agriculture. The 1930s being the decade of the Depression, little wage employment was available, and the markets for rugs and jewelry were not what they had been during the prosperous 1920s. Civilian Conservation Corps and other temporary government employment projects provided more than one-third of the Navajos' per capita income by 1937.

"Relative deprivation" experienced by many Navajo as a result of the government stock-reduction program induced one-seventh of the reservation Navajo to take up the Peyote religion, according to Aberle. Persons most likely to join the religion, he found, were those who had not only lost their stock, but suffered disturbing dreams as a consequence of their unhappiness. The closeness and mutual support of the Peyote religion congregations were therapeutic for these people, it seemed, and helped them resist falling into alcoholism in their despair.

Peyote had been around for decades before the stock-reduction program. It originally was a north-Mexican Indian religion using the peyote cactus, growing in the desert south of the Rio Grande, as a sacrament and means to induce visions in its priests. In the nineteenth century, Peyote was taken up by some Southwestern Indian groups bordering Mexico, and from them it passed to Indian Territory in Oklahoma.

By the early twentieth century, several versions of a peyote-using religion had developed, each with its own leader. Most of these incorporated some Christian symbolism, most noticeable in the claim that peyote was for the Indian what the Bible was for the European, God's chosen means of revelation. Bureau of Indian Affairs officials and Euro-American "friends of the Indian" campaigned to eradicate this "drug," although peyote is not addictive and many congregation members may take only a small bit as communion, not enough to cause mental effects. Indians fought back by legally incorporating a Native American Church of Peyote religionists and invoking Constitutional protection for the free exercise of religion. James Mooney had assisted them, bringing upon himself a vicious attack on his character from opponents of Indian religions. By 1920, the two sides had fought to a draw.

Peyote remained a common religion among American Indians in the West, including a few Navajos. It developed many variants, since the preferences of and revelations gained by every sincere leader are respected, but the basic religion combines a personal moral code, not unlike Jack Wilson's "clean, honest life," with night-long rituals in a tipi or hogan. A meeting is held when a member wishes the congregation to offer prayers for a loved one in ill health, distress, or danger. Peyote prayer meetings resemble the Round Plain

New Tidings meetings, with earth altars representing the world with a "road of life" drawn on them, and a communal meal closing the event. The principal difference between Peyote and Jack Wilson's religion is that Peyote never included an open-air dance and never was heralded as a means to resurrect the dead.

Aberle seemed to have a strong case for his argument that deprivation had driven one-seventh of the Navajo nation to the Peyote religion beginning in the mid-1930s. Navajo had not joined the Ghost Dance religion around 1890, when they saw their herds prospering and felt relatively comfortable. Peyote religion had been known and available to the Navajo for decades before it became relatively popular in the mid-1930s. It was the only religion then prevalent that would strengthen despairing Navajo in both commitment to moral behavior *and* confidence in the goodness of Navajo culture. That the Navajo were experiencing a "negative discrepancy between legitimate expectation [by anyone's standards of legitimacy] and actuality" is clearly documented, and so is the increase in commitment to a new religion.

Aberle's study of the first success of a non-Navajo Indian religion on the Navajo Reservation, the Peyote religion in the 1930s, seemed to explain the lack of success of Jack Wilson's proselytizers in 1889–1890. Aberle closely documented the material circumstances of the Navajo around 1890 and in succeeding decades, showing a clear contrast in the actual economic situations, as well as a contrast in Navajo morale, in 1890 compared with the years after stock reduction began in 1934. His success in accounting for Navajo scoffing at the Ghost Dance and then conversion to Peyote forty-five years later stimulated him to directly explain the general attraction of Jack Wilson's religion: "It is not my aim to contend that the Prophet Dance of the Northwest *is* a response to deprivation resulting from changes imposed by [European] contact. Rather, I wish to point out that it *could* be" (Aberle 1959:83).

Leslie Spier could not resist sharply rebutting, "Who, we may ask, has contended it couldn't?" (Spier, Suttles, & Herskovits 1959:88). "To state merely that deprivation *could* have been present—which is all he actually says—is undeniable. But this is scarcely helpful since it remains no more than an assumption until specific evidence is adduced" (Spier, Suttles, & Herskovits 1959:85).

Aberle did not answer this challenge by arraying the data on extinction of the bison herds and proselytization of the new religion in the Plains, data that would show a neat parallel to Navajo livestock deprivation and attraction to the Peyote religion. Had he done so, he would have seemed to strengthen his case for the causal relation between deprivation and new religions. The hypothesis nevertheless would not have held well for Jack Wilson and the Tövusi-dökadö, who had never been dependent upon bison and were not poorly off around 1889.

W. W. Hill was an anthropologist at the University of New Mexico who knew Navajo throughout the 1930s. He did not concur with Aberle's explanation for Navajo rejection of the Ghost Dance religion. To Hill, there was nothing comparable about Navajo reaction to the Paiute proselytizers in

1889–1890 and Navajo conversion to Peyote after 1934. Hill had a simple explanation for the failure of Jack Wilson's disciples: Navajo, like all Apachean (Navajo and Apaches are closely related) peoples, have a terrible fear of the dead. They traditionally destroyed all of a deceased person's belongings, would not speak his or her name, and moved camp to a new location, all so that the ghost would be unable to haunt them. The Paiutes came from the north, where the Navajo know the spirits of the dead are to be found. Navajo panicked, Hill was sure, when the Paiutes told them the dead would return.

Several Navajo who remembered 1889–1890 told Hill about the prophecies made at that time. One man said that many young people died soon afterward. Another man recalled, "The days were just hazy and the sun was reddish." Elderly Navajo warned at the time, "If they [the dead] come back it will mean that they will bring back all kinds of sickness. Also, if they come back there will be no rains and no corn" (quoted in Hill 1944:526). "Most of the people thought that this was started by the witches," an informant told Hill (1944:527).

Peyote religion has a positive appeal to many Navajo. Its teachers emphasize the therapeutic goodness of the rapport with God achieved by communion through the peyote cactus. Protected by this goodness, the believer is no longer tempted by alcohol, adultery, drugs, or suicide. Believers are also protected from such Navajo evils as witchcraft. Peyotists can participate in traditional Navajo ceremonies and in Christian church worship, if they wish. For some Navajo, Peyote syncretizes the three religions by offering a ritual functioning as an alternative or supplement to the traditional Blessing Way, through revelation explicitly parallel to that in the Christian Bible. Peyote mollifies, rather than excites, Navajo fear of the dead. During the distress experienced in the 1930s, Peyote amplified a Navajo's spiritual protection and thus might allay disturbing dreams.

Hill argued that the Ghost Dance and Peyote would have been perceived as radically different by Navajo, so that an explanation for the success, or lack of it, of one is irrelevant to explaining the other. His argument is "idealist"; Aberle's on "relative deprivation" is "materialist." Both working from firsthand experience among the Navajo, they each bring out significant factors. Washington Matthews corroborates Aberle's emphasis on the comfort enjoyed by the majority of Navajo around 1890 and the optimism most felt as the United States reimbursed them for the persecution they had suffered in the 1860s. Few had reason to be dissatisfied with their traditional religion. Hill's and Stephen's direct testimonies from Navajo make it clear that material satisfaction was only the background of Navajo rejection of Jack Wilson's religion. The "efficient cause," as philosophers would analyze it, was the promise of ghosts returning, a promise given by men who themselves came from the dead land in the north. If the Paiute preachers had soft-pedaled that line about the dead returning, if they had stressed Jack Wilson's reputation as a doctor, they might have had a few converts among the Navajo.

Manuelito was one of the most respected Navajo leaders around 1890. One of Hill's informants remembered Manuelito saying, " 'We know that ghosts are bad.' He tried to get the people to think of beneficial things, like agriculture and sheep raising. He said, 'Why ask the ghosts to come back; some day you will get a chance to go there' " (Hill 1944:526).

9/Revitalization

Ninety years before Jack Wilson went to heaven and returned with his message from God, a Seneca Iroquois chief titled Handsome Lake went the same journey. Handsome Lake's gospel became the foundation of an Iroquois religion still strong on the Iroquois reservations. Parallels abound between the two prophets, their circumstances, and their messages. Examining these parallels, we may finally perceive the common threads linking not only the Ghost Dance and the Iroquois Longhouse religions, but these with Black Elk, Peyote, and the contemporary Indian activism that exploded at Wounded Knee.

Handsome Lake is a title of leadership among the Seneca nation of Iroquois, whose homeland is western New York near Lake Erie. The man who bears the title Handsome Lake, selected for this office by the senior women of the Turtle Clan of the Seneca, represents the clan in the governing council of the Seneca, and is part of the delegation of "chiefs" (titleholders) representing the Seneca nation in the councils of the League of the Iroquois Nations. Probably about 1795, the matrons of the Turtle Clan chose for the office of Handsome Lake a man sixty years of age, nephew to the noted chief and diplomat Guyasuta, half-brother to the leader Cornplanter. The man would thenceforth be known by his title, *Skanyadariyoh*, "Handsome Lake."

During his lifetime, this Handsome Lake had seen his nation fall from a position of international power to bitter poverty. He was born in 1735. A few years earlier, the Seneca, with their sister nations in the League, the Cayuga, Onondaga, Oneida, and Mohawk, had welcomed into their long-standing alliance the Tuscarora, who had emigrated from North Carolina. The original Five Nations had defeated their major competitors, the Huron and the Petun, in the mid-seventeenth century and since then had dominated the fur trade and frontier politics from the St. Lawrence River through the Great Lakes, and south deep into the Ohio Valley.

The League had appeared in the protohistoric period, the sixteenth century, in western New York. A saintly stranger, Dekanawidah, came among the Iroquois fervently seeking to create peace among their constantly warring communities. Dekanawidah, who is said to have suffered from a speech impediment, recruited a Mohawk, Hiawatha, to travel around Iroquois country with him, delivering speeches describing the virtues of peace. At the principal town of the Onondaga, the prophet and his apostle faced the terrible

Figure 34. Cornplanter (Gaye'twahgeh), Seneca leader, painted in the early nineteenth century.

Thadodaho, a chief so fearsome his head spouted snakes. Hiawatha had himself been a fierce warrior, then was driven out of his mind with rage and sorrow when he returned from war to find his family murdered. Dekanawidah had encountered Hiawatha wandering in the forest like a cannibal monster. The prophet of peace had calmed the wild hermit, inspiring him to go out among the towns to help construct a better life for all the people. Thadodaho met his match in Hiawatha and the quiet Dekanawidah, whose beatific countenance was as beautiful as Thadodaho's was horrible. The epic confrontation between the warmonger and the peacemakers ended with Thadodaho resolving to devote all his energy to supporting the building of the League. To this day, the chairman of the great council of the League bears the title Thadodaho.

For two-thirds of the eighteenth century, the Iroquois were the critical factor in the affairs of many nations—British, Dutch, French, and Indian—in northeastern America. The geographical position of the Five Nations of the Iroquois along the western frontier of the American colonies, on the major routes to the interior, allowed the Iroquois to act as gatekeepers and toll-takers in international trade. Their position was strengthened by their economic development. The subsistence of the communities was based on agriculture, which was efficiently carried out in the rich valleys of western New York by cooperative work groups of women, each group consisting of the women of a matrilineal clan who lived with their husbands and children in apartments under a common roof, the longhouse. This close cooperation in daily living allowed the men of the clans to leave the villages once they had done the heavy labor of preparing the fields in spring and again once they had assisted in the fall harvest. The women of the matrilineages cared for each other, the children, and the elderly. The men were away for months at a time, trading and hunting sometimes hundreds of miles from their own towns. Thanks to Dekanawidah, they had little fear that their families would be destroyed as Hiawatha's had been, for no Iroquois would break the peace of the League against a sister nation, and other Indians knew they were courting sure devastation by the allied armies of the League if they dared attack a League town.

Matters changed in the 1760s. France and Britain, maneuvering for a century-and-a-half to gain dominance in North America, finally fought to a showdown in the Seven Years' War, called the French and Indian War in America, from 1756 to 1763. Victory went to Britain. For over a century, Iroquois had functioned as the third party in the balance of power in northeastern America; now, there was no balance, only Britain. Without the possibility of giving and receiving military and economic assistance with France, the Iroquois could no longer challenge British hegemony. Homesteaders from the thirteen colonies moved through the traditional frontier along the Appalachians into the valleys of western Pennsylvania and Ohio, safer now that British forts stood in the Northwest Territory.

For two-thirds of the eighteenth century, the Iroquois had shone as treaty makers. The League of the Five Nations was itself, after all, a treaty constructed by Dekanawidah. Iroquois participated in dozens of treaties as parties or as diplomats facilitating the negotiations of other parties. Many of these treaties were printed, thirteen of them by Benjamin Franklin as part of his business as a commercial printer. (Later, Franklin used what he had thus learned of Iroquois governance structure, in 1753 when he was a member of Pennsylvania's delegation to a treaty council with Iroquois at Carlisle, and then as a model of confederated democratic republics. He interested Thomas Jefferson in appealing to the Iroquois Confederacy as an example of government respectful of each citizen's inalienable right to life, liberty, and the pursuit of happiness, but not of the accumulation of private property at the cost of beggaring others.)

The outbreak of hostilities between American colonists and Britain in 1775 underscored the radical change in the balance of power that followed the defeat of France in 1763. Both the rebels and British wanted Iroquois allies, but neither would court Iroquois favor as the French and British had done earlier. Some Iroquois sided with Britain, particularly many Mohawks close to Sir William Johnson, an English trader and then Britain's Superintendent of Indian Affairs, who had married into a prominent Mohawk matrilineage. Other Iroquois were willing to fight with the rebels. A large number of Iroquois tried to be neutral. The dissension within the League caused the Thadodaho and his fellow League chiefs to suspend the League for the duration of the war.

The Treaty of Paris that formally settled the American Revolution in 1783 ignored American Indians. Each Iroquois nation had to negotiate its relationship with the new United States or abandon its New York villages to take up land grants under British rule in Canada. Iroquois nations were all divided, and the League itself divided between those who would reconstitute it among the Canadian settlements and those who insisted it must remain in its New York homeland. Those Iroquois who would not give up their ancestral country accepted reservations from the United States; having no real choice after the devastation wreaked upon much of their land during the war, they also agreed to sell or cede most of their prewar territories.

Postwar life on the Iroquois reservations in New York was miserable. The Iroquois men found themselves unemployed: They had lost the advantages they once had as traders, their hunting grounds were being turned into American farms, and once they had built cabin homes and cleared fields for the women of their matrilineages there was no proper men's work for them on the reservations. What there was, it seemed, and was in great quantity was liquor. Drinking became the common occupation of too many men, and drinking too often climaxed in brawls and rampages through the villages. Men seemed bewitched, a criminal charge among the Iroquois who believed in the reality of sorcery.

Handsome Lake was not immune to the demoralization of his people. In 1796, about the time he himself had been raised to the office of Handsome Lake, his half-brother Cornplanter was given a grant of land near, but outside of, the Allegany Seneca Reservation. It was a reward from the State of Pennsylvania for persuading the Seneca to avoid allying with the Indians west of the mountains who had been fighting colonist invaders until they were defeated in 1794. Handsome Lake, who apparently was a widower at this time, moved to the grant with his married daughter and her family, into a cabin adjacent to Cornplanter's. In 1798, Quakers from Philadelphia began a mission with the Allegany Seneca, starting a school to teach the Indian children English and literacy, and a model farm to demonstrate the superiority of European-style farming (and the propriety of men taking full responsibility for farming).

For some years, Cornplanter had been suggesting that the people of his band make more of an effort to adapt to the modern ways of their Euro-American neighbors. He invited a millwright to operate a mill on his grant, until the man turned out to be mostly interested in quick money from bootlegging whiskey. Finding honest friends who would not take advantage of the Indians' limited knowledge of English and the American legal system handicapped those of Cornplanter's people wishing to add more Euro-American technology to their repertoire. The energetic, passionately sincere young Quaker missionaries proved to be the kind of friends Cornplanter wanted, and after several trials of the young men, he supported their efforts.

Handsome Lake was more conservative than his half-brother. During the winter of 1798–1799, he had been out for months with a party of families hunting along the Allegheny River. Deer were plentiful, and the families amassed a good quantity of dried meat and hides. At the end of the season, in April, Handsome Lake and the men rafted down to Pittsburgh to trade the surplus from their catch, while the women packed meat back to the village. In May, the men appeared. The take from the winter's hunt had bought plenty of kegs of whiskey. The trip from Pittsburgh had been an extended carouse, which did not end once the men were home. For several weeks, the men, including Handsome Lake, continued to drink. Their families hid out in the bush as the drunks kicked in cabin doors, vandalized homes, and beat each other up. Neglected, hungry dogs yelped and cried.

Cornplanter, his council of representatives from the families of his band, and the missionaries decreed prohibition on whiskey, appointing two young men to organize people for constructive activities. The drinking ceased, mostly because the supply brought from Pittsburgh had run out. Some of the men were willing to follow the European pattern of men working in the fields while women tended to house and barnyard chores. The Quakers plowed fields for these men, using the mission's team and plow. Other, younger Seneca men worked as laborers on the mission farm or on building a schoolhouse to replace the small cabin first assigned to the mission school.

Whether from the prolonged drinking bout or the effects of a winter hunting, Handsome Lake, who was in his sixties, became ill and kept to his bed in June 1799. Morning and night, he prayed that he might survive and daily thanked the Creator for his life. On June 15, he staggered out of bed to the door of his cabin, then collapsed. His daughter, working just outside, ran and caught him. He seemed cold, not breathing. Her husband hurriedly brought Cornplanter and his (and Handsome Lake's) nephew Blacksnake to assist. Both half-brother and nephew noticed that the unconscious man's chest remained warm, so they sat with him in the house until, two hours later, he came to himself again.

But it was not the same man who awoke from . . . a trance? Handsome Lake revealed that his soul had left his body at the door of the cabin to attend

Figure 35. Handsome Lake preaching, drawn a century later by a Seneca artist using his contemporary congregation as a model.

three men beautifully clothed in Indian dress, who were messengers from the Creator. They imposed upon him the duty to preach the next day at the annual Strawberry Festival, when the people thanked their Creator for the bounty of early summer. Handsome Lake must warn the people against four evils: whiskey, witchcraft, love magic, and potions used to induce abortion or sterility. The next day was not soon enough for this message to be conveyed. At Handsome Lake's suggestion, Cornplanter called the whole community to come hear, and since the prophet himself was too weak to repeat the message before the large gathering, his half-brother retold it. The Quakers, who had come over with the rest of the people, were deeply impressed as Cornplanter's son (who had been to school in Philadelphia) translated the divine message for them.

Handsome Lake affirmed to the community the evilness of much that had been troubling them for a long time. Indeed, only three months before, a young man of the band had returned from hunting to recount a dream he had experienced, in which he had seemed unable to remain in a house with a beautiful, kindly man presiding, but went to a dismal place where he suffered punishment for his drinking, adultery, and wife beating. This young man vowed to reform himself. Handsome Lake spoke reform to the whole community.

Two months later, on August 7, 1799, Handsome Lake awoke from dreaming of an angel, like the three who had brought him the Creator's message in June. All day, Handsome Lake, dressed in his best, sat with Cornplanter awaiting the angel. As night fell, Handsome Lake went into an hour-long trance in the course of which his soul was led by the four angels up along the Milky Way (the road dead souls take). Like the Italian poet Dante in his *Divine Comedy*, Handsome Lake recounted observing scenes from purgatory, from hell, and, at last, from heaven. Along the way, he met George Washington, resting with his dog on a comfortable veranda, and Jesus, who sorrowfully told of his execution and advised the Indians "that they will become lost when they follow the ways of the white man." (This was from Handsome Lake's own account taken down by the Quaker missionary on August 10.) The fourth angel instructed him to return to preach again to the Iroquois, to emphasize to them the importance of living together in harmony and worshipping their Creator in their traditional manner.

Half a year later, on February 5, 1800, the original three angels came back to Handsome Lake to inquire whether his people had reformed according to the first prophetic vision. Were whiskey and witchcraft banished from the Indian communities? The prophet admitted he could not be sure. His divine visitors once more laid upon him the burden of preaching the gospel in which he had been instructed. Iroquois were to lead a clean, honest life and continue to honor the ways of their own culture.

Cornplanter and the brothers' half-sister Gayantgogwus, most knowledgeable of the Seneca doctors and spokeswoman for the women of the community, both supported Handsome Lake. So, too, did the man who led the prayers and homilies at the community's major ceremonies of worship. By the autumn of 1800, Handsome Lake was in a position of considerable power, enjoying not only the assistance of these leaders in promulgating the reforms he must enact, but also gifted, through another visit by the angels, with the ability to see hidden evil. With this, he fingered witches who were causing illness. One of these accusations almost brought about war between the Seneca and their usual allies the Munsee (Delaware), Handsome Lake claiming that a Munsee witch was killing Cornplanter's daughter, who had just borne a child to a young Munsee leader. Supposedly, the father did not want to marry his child's Seneca mother and engaged a sorcerer to get rid of her. The Munsee, of course, staunchly denied the accusation and, to show their good faith, sent one of their most respected doctors to treat the young woman.

Cornplanter's daughter did not die, yet harmony was not restored. In June 1801, Seneca met in council to discuss selling parcels of their land: Handsome Lake's nephew Red Jacket, official speaker of the Seneca council, led the faction in favor of selling land to New York State. Handsome Lake opposed selling land as a thing morally wrong in itself, as well as unwise. He declared that his four angel instructors had revealed to him the evilness of the proposed sale and shown him Red Jacket toiling in hell for the sin. The June council postponed decision on the sale, while applauding Handsome Lake's urging the prohibition of liquor and placing on record their naming the prophet "High Priest, and principal Sachem" (chief).

Considering that the angels taught peace and harmony in the community as the wish of the Creator, Handsome Lake could not adamantly oppose those

Seneca who advocated more accommodation to the American colonists surrounding them. By November 1801, the land sales had gone through, in exchange for benefits to be paid the Seneca by the federal government. That winter, Handsome Lake joined leaders of the other League nations (except Mohawk) and Munsee in a formal delegation to President Thomas Jefferson in Washington. Handsome Lake greeted Jefferson as his equivalent, principal Sachem of the American nation. The Seneca prophet, it now appeared, had been appointed to extend the teaching of the gospel given him to the Americans, through their President. Handsome Lake apologized for delaying bringing the gospel to the Americans until he had preached it to his own Seneca people. Jefferson took the prophet's speech in the spirit in which it was intended, and in a written reply highly commended Handsome Lake's gospel—though without acknowledging its application to Euro-Americans.

In 1804, Handsome Lake led a number of families to build a new village at Cold Spring Creek on the Senecas' Allegany reservation just north of Cornplanter's grant. The Quaker missionaries tried to persuade the Seneca to disperse onto individual family farms in the Euro-American pattern, but Handsome Lake explained that the community's homes must be close together in a village in order to carry out the midwinter religious ceremonies. Techniques of farming, seeds and stock, implements, mills, blacksmithing, spinning, and weaving could all be assimilated from the American culture into nineteenth-century Iroquois life; Handsome Lake did not discourage changes in material culture. Religion, however, must continue according to the revelations made to the Iroquois in ancient times and in visions since. Religion and social organization were intertwined, each supporting the other. Each needed the land to maintain the community, the congregation. Handsome Lake could not let the land base of the Seneca be chipped away, for that would undermine the people's capacity to carry on the Iroquois life ordained by their Creator.

As would happen with Jack Wilson late in the century, Handsome Lake led the renewed commitment of Indian people to their heritage by himself traveling to other reservations to preach and by receiving pilgrims at his own village. His constant reminders to worship the creator and to avoid drinking, quarreling, witchcraft, adultery, and wife beating were reinforced by his reporting, from time to time, additional visitations from his attendant angels. All the Iroquois and allied Indian nations became familiar with his gospel and looked up to him as truly a "principal Sachem." During the War of 1812, Handsome Lake urgently advised Indians to stay out of the fighting. Opposed to Tecumseh and his prophet brother Tenskwatawa, Shawnee leaders of an Indian alliance against the United States, Handsome Lake was called the Peace Prophet.

Handsome Lake died on August 10, 1815, at the council house of the Onondaga, the traditional heart of the League of the Iroquois. He had come to preach and counsel his many disciples. Though his sage advice, on tribal business matters as well as on personal and religious problems, would be

Figure 36. Chiefs of the Six Nations of the League of the Iroquois, 1871. The chiefs are displaying the wampum belts commemorating the major treaties of their nations.

sorely missed, he had strengthened a younger generation, of which his nephew Blacksnake was a leader, to carry on as Iroquois. A newspaper in the American town of Buffalo, bordering Iroquois settlements, noted in an obituary of the prophet, "From a filthy, lazy, drunken set of beings, [the Iroquois] have become cleanly, industrious, sober, and happy" (quoted in Wallace 1969:321). From the utter demoralization of defeat and devastation, Handsome Lake inspired the peoples of the League to rebuild their lives, faithful to their communities and heritage. His gospel is still recited today in the longhouses of the Iroquois reservations—as Henry Two Bears recited the gospel of Jack Wilson's religion at Round Plain—and the congregations still feel the inspiration Handsome Lake carried to them.

REVITALIZATION MOVEMENTS

An anthropologist, Anthony F. C. Wallace, was deeply impressed by the story of the prophet Handsome Lake. Wallace's father, Paul Wallace, was a historian who had published a study of the League of the Five Nations. Anthony Wallace realized that Handsome Lake had led the Iroquois out of the devastation and despair of war much as had Dekanawidah in legendary times. Anthony Wallace studied the documents on Handsome Lake (the Quaker missionaries, happily, had kept voluminous journals of the events they witnessed) and also observed and talked with the Iroquois of today. He analyzed the process of "revitalization" crystallized by Handsome Lake, suggesting it can be seen as a model of "revitalization movements" that seem to regularly fall into these phases (Wallace 1956):

I. *Period of generally satisfactory adaptation* to a group's social and natural environment. For the Iroquois, this would describe the seventeenth and most of the eighteenth century.

II. *Period of increased individual stress.* The group as a whole can survive through its accustomed cultural behavior, but changes in the social or natural environment (e.g., military defeat, epidemics, famine) frustrate the efforts of many persons to obtain normal satisfactions of their needs. For the Iroquois, this would have been the period between 1763 and 1776, when the Iroquois had lost their political advantage as the third force in the balance of power between Britain and France.

III. *Period of cultural distortion.* Changes in the group's social or natural environment drastically reduce the capacity of accustomed cultural behavior to satisfy most persons' physical and emotional needs. For the Iroquois, this would have been between 1776 and 1799, when American army raids had ruined their homes and fields and they were driven either to small reservations or to colonies in Canada. The curtailment of the traditional Iroquois economy employing men as long-distance traders and hunters left the male population largely un- or underemployed, interfered with the women's accustomed work patterns, and left many seeking relief through destructive indulgence in drinking, venting anger through witchcraft, and sexual promiscuity (Handsome Lake's warnings against using potions for love magic and abortion were aimed at curbing promiscuity).

IV. *Period of revitalization:* (1) reformulation of the cultural pattern, (2) its communication, (3) organization of a reformulated cultural pattern, (4) adaptation of the reformulated pattern to better meet the needs and preferences of the group, (5) cultural transformation, (6) routinization—the adapted reformulated cultural pattern becomes the standard cultural behavior for the group. For the Iroquois, this would be from Handsome Lake's first visions, 1799, to the 1830s.

V. *New period of generally satisfactory adaptation* to the group's changed social and/or natural environment. For the Iroquois, this would be from about the end of the 1830s to the present.

Parallels between Handsome Lake and Jack Wilson become clear if Wallace's model of revitalization is applied to analysis of their movements. Period I for the Tövusi-dökadö was their aboriginal culture up to about 1860, when Euro-American colonists appeared. Period II was about 1860 to the 1880s. Period III, cultural distortion, was the 1880s, with the expansion of agribusiness in Walker River Valley and increasing imposition of United States governance, for example, by instituting courts with judges beginning 1883, and formal schooling in 1887. Note that none of these factors had drastic consequences: It was the accumulation of changes that by the late 1880s had distorted the traditional Tövusi-dökadö cultural pattern. Period IV began, of course, with the revelation of the new gospel to Jack Wilson in 1889 and continued to about 1900. Period V began about 1900, when Walker River Valley was completely dominated by agribusiness development, the rabbits nearly exterminated, fish severely depleted by irrigation canal barriers, and the Paiutes superficially assimilated into the margin of American society but unobtrusively maintaining the basic tenets of their culture. By articulating a reformulated cultural pattern, Jack Wilson had forestalled the loss of Paiute culture.

Comparing Handsome Lake and Jack Wilson, we see that cultural distortion is not inevitably precipitous and dramatic. Iroquois losses had been rapid and disastrous; Tövusi-dökadö, gradual and incremental. Iroquois were despairing, at each other's throats quarreling over what course of action to take. Tövusi-dökadö maintained a strong community spirit and tolerant attitude toward each other and toward outsiders. Handsome Lake truly revitalized the Iroquois. Whether the Tövusi-dökadö ought to be described as undergoing revitalization with Jack Wilson might be debated, for they never felt deathly despair as the Iroquois had. Anthony Wallace chose his term, "revitalization," after studying Iroquois history. If he had instead studied Jack Wilson's religion in its Nevada homeland, he might have termed the process of culture change "reformulation" rather than "revitalization."

The wisdom of asserting that Jack Wilson's religion was a "revitalization movement" fully comparable to Handsome Lake's appears when we look at the spread of the Ghost Dance religion. On the Plains, it was absolutely revitalizing. Alexander Lesser's study of the Pawnee described a people as devastated as the Iroquois, and similarly resuscitated by a prophet's vision. Lakota, too, were revitalized. That was perceived as threatening by the agents and homesteaders who moved onto the half of the Great Sioux Reservation just taken away from the Sioux by the United States government. The Sioux were supposed to be beaten, not requickened.

Black Elk took upon himself, at this time, the burden of reformulating his people's culture. He assumed he could discover the critical elements for a revitalized society by observing urban Americans and Europeans. These were certainly vigorous peoples, held up as models to the Lakota. Decades of following a reformulated cultural pattern as a Lakota Catholic catechist was, in the end, less than satisfactory to Black Elk's emotional and even physical needs: Christianity remained incomplete to him as a religious system, and he and his people were mired in great poverty. He turned back to his ancestral religion, reformulating it into a structure reminiscent of Catholicism but incorporating fundamental Lakota values and symbols. Black Elk's apostles Neihardt and Brown illustrate an aspect of the reformulation process mentioned by Wallace—adaptation. Both modified the prophet's actual dictates to make them more easily understood by, and more consonant with, their intended audience, Euro-Americans.

As with Jack Wilson's Ghost Dance, the twentieth-century history of the Lakota, including Black Elk, amplifies and clarifies the model of cultural reformulation, or "revitalization," developed by Anthony Wallace. The period of cultural distortion need not be precipitous or devastating; it was for the Iroquois, the Lakota, the Navajo, but not for the Tövusi-dökadö. The reformulation, accordingly, may be dramatically revitalizing, or simply sustaining. What counts is that the culmination of the process remains cultural transformation, as marked in Walker River Valley as at Cold Spring, New

York, or among the Pawnee. Without change, adaptation, reformulation, revitalization, transformation (call it what you will), a society—Indian, European, *any* society—cannot continue.

For the Tövusi-dökadö, reformulation seems to have staved off despair. After 1896, a number of Tövusi-dökadö, though never Jack Wilson, bought opium from Chinese laborers in Walker River Valley. Paiute users, like the Chinese who sold them the drug, came to depend upon opium for relaxation after long hours of wearying work. These Paiutes earned their living in the potato fields that took over much of Walker River Valley by 1900. Opium was no longer used by the Indians after 1934. Peyote was introduced to them in 1936 and was accepted as a spiritual medicine for persons suffering illness. Jack Wilson's long career doctoring, like Handsome Lake's sixteen years of ministering to his people after his vision, reminds us that the prophet himself is likely to be routinized, in Wallace's term, to become part of the transformed culture he or she catalyzed. Twentieth-century Walker River Paiutes—they could no longer be "the tövusi eaters"—maintained a cultural pattern that, like that of the Iroquois after Handsome Lake, placed them among, but not lost in, the enveloping Euro-American landscape. As the Iroquois have been vigorously asserting in recent years, these peoples remain distinct, if small, nations.

Nick Black Elk did not, after all, lead his people through cultural transformation, though he was one of many endeavoring to complete this. He himself felt that he had been detoured by Christianity, that, in retrospect, he had made a false turn and failed to remain true to his prophetic vision. He believed that if he had not erred in this way, perhaps he could have led a reformulation that would have revitalized the Lakota. Their cultural pattern had been transformed in his lifetime, but too much was imposed by alien authorities. Pine Ridge after World War I resembled the Iroquois reservations after the American Revolution—too much drinking, too much casual sex, too much factionalism, too little rewarding work.

Can a period of cultural distortion last for decades? The Oglala seem to demonstrate that continued frustration of efforts to build a self-sustaining economic base adversely affects cultural reformulation. Lakota religion persists (in spite of Nick Black Elk's years as a catechist), and the Oglala as a people survive; yet on the Sioux reservations the mood is still one of seeking a viable, satisfying pattern for life as Lakota. This may be found soon. Lakota religious ceremonies, from community Sun Dances of thanksgiving and renewal, to family memorial rites for loved ones, have been proliferating since the 1970s. The tribe operates a community college, Sinte Gleska, on Rosebud Reservation. Partially funded by Congress under a 1978 law, the college works to upgrade reservation residents' formal education and marketable skills *and* to teach Lakota arts, medicine, and religion. Interestingly, one-quarter of the students in the Lakota programs have been non-Indian, many of them no doubt drawn by reading the Black Elk books. Coupled with aggressive legal action to recover the Sioux claim in the Black Hills, Sinte Gleska College may be part of a revitalization of the Lakota, what Wounded Knee in 1973 was meant to be.

When John Collier agreed with the Corps of Engineers that erosion on the Navajo Reservation was "Public Enemy No. 1," cultural distortion intensified among the Navajo. They had been managing for decades much like the Tövusi-dökadö, in a long period of individual stress increased from what it had been before confrontation with the United States, but not to the point of wholesale cultural distortion. Destroying the flocks of the poorer families on the reservation created that distortion. Traditional patterns of subsistence became impossible for a sizable segment of the tribe. The despairing seemed ready to turn to alcoholism and immorality, as the Iroquois had. Peyote was available for the Navajo, having developed as cultural reformulation by neighboring Indian peoples half a century earlier. To say, as Aberle did, that "relative deprivation" converted one-seventh of the Navajo nation to peyote tells only part of the story of cultural reformulation, just as Hill's assertion that fear of the dead kept the Navajo out of the Ghost Dance is only part of the story. In 1889, Navajo had a distinctly successful cultural pattern. After 1934, poorer Navajo suffered under cultural distortion and many sought reformulation. Peyote was one "road"; other Navajo tried to work a pattern of wage work more fully into Navajo culture.

The American Indian Movement originated in a period of cultural distortion afflicting both Indians on economically depressed reservations and those in the cities. Dennis Banks, the Bellecourt brothers, and Russell Means happened to have respectable jobs in 1968, but they and their friends had experienced discrimination, jail, poverty, and alcohol abuse. The cultural pattern of behavior taught them by middle-class Euro-Americans tended to fail in the face of racial discrimination. So did their attempts to live on reservations. Some, of mixed ancestry, could pass for Euro-American and avoid discrimination, but that brought guilt at denying their Indian parentage. Others, physically more obviously Indian, could not avoid discrimination and the poverty it often entailed. Indians needed to formulate a cultural pattern that maintained the core of their Indian heritage without costing them material comfort and security. Civil rights reform in the 1960s held out a promise that, at last, racial discrimination might no longer hinder Indian achievement.

AIM leaders tried to work out such a reformulation. In an era when "Power to the People!" was a popular slogan, they put that into their reformulation. The "Bureau Machine" should give political and economic power back to the Indians, something Carlos Montezuma and his associates had called for fifty years earlier, and John Collier had intended in 1934. A reformulation couched in purely secular terms failed to satisfy AIM leaders and many of their potential followers. They recruited Leonard Crow Dog to add a spiritual dimension to their reformulation that would legitimatize their "vision" as the messages from the Creator had legitimatized the reformulations and leadership of Handsome Lake and Jack Wilson—and, much less successfully, Black Elk.

Handsome Lake had been fortunate that the United States president to whom he revealed his gospel was the extraordinary Thomas Jefferson, himself a prophet reaping the fruits of the cultural reformulation he had led by means of the Declaration of Independence and the United States Constitution. Jefferson had legitimatized that reformulation by appealing to the "inalienable rights" endowed by our Creator, and he easily approved of his Seneca fellow prophet who similarly claimed the Creator's support. In 1933, there was another president, Franklin Roosevelt, who favored cultural reformulation (the New Deal), but let Collier, a non-Indian, act as prophet for the Indians. Collier, not surprisingly, reformulated Euro-American rather than any Indian cultural pattern, and in reaction thousands of Navajo turned to the peyote road. The United States presidents in 1890 and 1968–1973 were, unfortunately, very ordinary mortals who saw Indian cultural reformulation as rebellion deserving crushing by military force.

Cultural reformulation necessarily occurs over and over again in every society. Neither natural nor social circumstances ever remain truly stable, though some aspects change very slowly. Societies must modify their customary patterns of behavior to take account of changes in their resources, their population, and the other societies with which they must deal. In this, the evolution of societies is little different from the evolution of biological organisms, the populations of which similarly are modified as environmental changes favor certain capabilities over others. This is not a matter of "progress" but of adaptation to necessity; there is no single line of development but a multitude of adaptations.

European empire building has given us the idea that European nations, and their emigrants overseas, represent the most "progressive," farthest evolved societies, superior to the native peoples of other continents. This self-serving notion began in English colonial policy in the seventeenth century. Governor John Winthrop of Massachusetts Bay Colony in 1629, and John Locke for the British Board of Trade in 1689, articulated the dictum that land not fenced and plowed by a private proprietor was *vacuum domicilium*, "empty" or "waste." They appealed to the Bible, Genesis 1:28, to claim that God ordered men to "subdue" and "replenish" the earth, and that anyone who failed to do so by fencing and plowing had forfeited any right to the land. By this argument, English peasants lost their villages' common pastures, the Scots and the Irish lost most of their countries, and Africa and America were held to be legitimately open to European usurpation.

In the eighteenth century, European philosophers wrote histories of mankind (women were thought to be of no historical importance), claiming four stages of human development from primitive hunting through herding of livestock and then agriculture, to the "Age of Commerce" in which they lived. These histories, with meager factual basis, functioned as myths explaining the contemporary state of the world as God's plan. The writers claimed to be scientists concerned with truth, yet in 1755—after, for example, Benjamin Franklin had published the Iroquois materials that so impressed him—a popular book stated of the Indians, "*America* may . . . be called the

. . . meanest of Mankind; no Civil Government, no Religion, no Letters; the *French* call them *Les Hommes des Bois*, or Men-Brutes of the Forrest [the French phrase translates 'Men of the Forest'—nothing about 'Brutes']" (William Douglass, quoted in Meek 1976:137).

Nineteenth-century Europeans and Euro-Americans, still bent on asserting that Manifest Destiny justified their wars of colonization, continued such propaganda. Lewis Henry Morgan wrote a book on the Iroquois when many who knew Handsome Lake were still alive, and concluded, "Indian life is . . . a negative state, without inherent vitality, and without powers of resistance" (Morgan [1851] 1954:108). Even a twentieth-century anthropologist who had studied Iroquois wrote in a textbook, "Primitive culture patterns are set in a rigid frame. . . . The material equipment of a group persists by its own inertia . . . each growing generation simply finds these objects there to be picked up where they were left by their fathers" (Goldenweiser 1937:407).

This myth of "the primitive" denied the reality of American Indian nations and their cultures, and obscured the reformulations by which they have maintained themselves. After the occupation of Alcatraz, in the year of the Trail of Broken Treaties march on Washington, a publisher would still set in print, "It was the Great Ghost Dance of 1890 . . . that provided the crashing climax to the collapse of American Indian culture. . . . [The 1890] Battle of Wounded Knee . . . was the last time that any considerable body of Indians in North America ever sought to threaten their new masters" (La Barre 1972:229, 232). This is part of a tradition of misinterpretation, including an often-cited paper by the sociologist Bernard Barber contrasting Jack Wilson's Ghost Dance to peyote: "The Peyote cult crystallized around passive acceptance and resignation in the face of the existing deprivation. It is an alternative response which seems better adapted to the existing phase of acculturation" (Barber 1941a:668).

The United States *wanted* Indians to be passive and resigned before their new masters, to be a vanishing race. The United States inherited from its European forebears a powerful predilection to justify conquest and oppression of smaller nations by describing them as godless, primitive, rigid, and without inherent vitality. American Indians have defied nearly five centuries of wars, virulent epidemics sometimes deliberately propagated, scorched-earth policies, and denial of human rights. Many Indian nations were killed off or forced to merge with others, losing their distinct identities. The majority have persisted by reformulating their cultural patterns, again and again, adapting many facets of their culture to the circumstances imposed upon them without losing the core of their beliefs and values. Often it has been a "prophet" articulating the reformulated pattern as a gospel that revitalized the community.

10/That Night in the Cabin

James Mooney jounced over the snowy desert in a wagon. I drove along sandy ruts through dense jackpine separating the North Saskatchewan River from the clearings of Round Plain. My sleepy three-year-old nestled close beside me. Our guide was Joe Douquette, a middle-aged Cree living just outside the small city of Prince Albert, Saskatchewan. Joe would introduce me to his wife's brother, Robert Goodvoice, and their stepfather, Henry Two Bears. Goodvoice, Two Bears, and Florence Douquette were Wahpeton Dakota Sioux and Round Plain Reserve. Mr. Two Bears would tell me something, the Douquettes promised.

It began . . . let's see. That evening, at Mabel Richards' house? No, before that. When I had met Mrs. Richards the summer before, at Lac La Ronge in the Saskatchewan bush? When Mrs. Richards had started the craft cooperative? When do the complicated skeins of real life have a beginning?

For me, it began in 1960. My husband and I were graduate students in anthropology at Harvard, both of us concentrating on the archaeology of North America. Tom, my husband, was juggling the last requirements for his Ph.D. with the demands of an exciting new job, the first full-time Provincial Archaeologist for Saskatchewan. I juggled the care of Tom, housework, and our little boy with my Ph.D. requirements. We each planned to excavate a Saskatchewan archaeological site and write it up for a dissertation: Tom would work at a bison drive near Gull Lake; I would work on François' House, the first successful fur trade post in the province. We presented our plans to our professor at Harvard. "Ah, but," he said to me, "you'll have to do something other than archaeology, something different from what Tom will do. Something in ethnology." "But . . . but . . . why?" I stammered. "Because otherwise people will think Tom did your dissertation for you."

No use asking, "What people would think that?" No use pointing out that Tom would be fully occupied with the work of a major prehistoric site several hours' drive from my proposed project. No use reminding the professor that we had scrupulously worked independently during the three years we had been at Harvard. Women, especially married women, *especially* married women with a child, were looked upon suspiciously by graduate school professors in 1960, three years before Betty Friedan's landmark feminist book would appear. There was no recourse. I would have to find some research topic wholly different from anything my husband might do.

So it was 1961, and I was looking about for anthropological research suitable for a dissertation, something I could pursue in Saskatchewan while minding my little boy (archaeology is good in that way—a site is a big sandbox for little kids). Someone mentioned having heard that a Ghost Dance shirt had been offered for sale in Prince Albert, the small northern city. Odd— the Ghost Dance religion was supposed to have been confined to the United States.

I drove up to Prince Albert. Mabel Richards might know about the shirt, and she was likely to suggest some topic in any case. Mabel was married to a geologist working in the Saskatchewan northern forest. Accompanying her husband on some of his field trips, she saw the Indian women making beautiful baskets, moccasins, and other crafts, selling them cheaply to the outfitters running fishing camps for rich sportsmen. There were no other outlets for the craftwork. There wasn't even a dirt road past Lac La Ronge settlement. Mabel Richards, believing strongly in socialist ethics (Saskatchewan had a locally developed socialist government then), determined to help the Indian women by organizing a craft cooperative and merchandising their work at a shop she would open in Prince Albert.

I had met Mabel Richards the summer before, when Tom and I, and our little boy, had spent some days at La Ronge, examining prehistoric sites reported by a conservation officer stationed there. Mabel had been pleased at my admiration for her project, and I was fascinated by her deep knowledge of the Indian peoples around Prince Albert and La Ronge, the transition zone between the prairies of southern Saskatchewan and the northern boreal forest. When I walked into her shop on a side street in Prince Albert in 1961, Mabel remembered me at once and greeted me warmly.

She had not seen, or heard of, any shirt resembling my description (from Mooney's monograph) of Ghost Dance shirts. She had not heard about this Ghost Dance ritual, or religion, whatever it was. Maybe I could research the crafts traditions for my study. Well, I should look around the shop, and why not come for supper to her house? Her husband was away in the field; it would just be her kids, mine, and us. We could have a good talk.

At suppertime, I pulled up beside her house on the outskirts of town. A tent was set up next to a large vegetable garden near the house. Mabel came out to greet me, then called to a middle-aged Indian couple at the tent. She introduced us—Joe and Florence Douquette; they were camping for the summer at her place, tending her vegetables. Did Mr. or Mrs. Douquette know anything about a shirt supposed to protect people, probably Sioux people, from bullets? A shirt worn in a special ritual dance called the Ghost Dance? In the 1890s? Part of a religion taught by a man named Wovoka or, in English, Jack Wilson? The Douquettes looked at each other. They slowly shook their heads "no."

It was dark when I left Mabel Richards' house. As I opened the car door, the Douquettes came up. They had something to say. They had been thinking about my questions. They had been thinking about how grateful they were to Mabel Richards, about how many times she had helped them and other

Indian people, about how difficult it was for people like them to reciprocate her generosity. If they helped her friend, she would understand it was done for her sake. They had talked this over with Florence's brother, and he agreed. As a gift, a gift of great value to Mabel Richards, they would tell her friend about Jack Wilson's religion. A friend welcomed into Mabel Richards' house could be trusted.

Thus, late that evening, I was driving with the Douquettes along the sandy ruts into Round Plain. The headlights picked out a log cabin in a clearing: Henry Two Bears' house. Mr. Two Bears, in his eighties, was the leader of the New Tidings congregation. Robert Goodvoice, Florence's brother, would interpret for Mr. Two Bears, who spoke only Dakota. (Many elderly Indians would speak only their own language, as a matter of pride, though they might understand English. On this evening, Mr. Two Bears would be recounting spiritual knowledge that he and others believed must be told exclusively in Dakota, lest mistranslation distort the vital message.)

We sat around the plain wooden table in the simple cabin lighted by a kerosene lamp. Everything—the cabin, its sparse furnishings, the off-the-beaten-track isolation of Round Plain, the buckboard wagons in yards, the old-fashioned country clothing of the people—could have been seen by James Mooney. I felt as if I had driven fifty years back in time, not eight miles from Prince Albert. Remembering how often popular historians and sociologists such as Barber had dismissed the Ghost Dance as a short-lived aberration, I was afraid that if I did not hold my breath, all might disappear as a dream.

Mr. Two Bears began explaining to me, in Dakota, how the religion of the Round Plain Dakota had been brought to them by Fred Robinson. He pointed to a framed photograph on the cabin wall, showing a handsome man in full Sioux costume; Robinson remained a real presence in the cabin. Then the old man announced he would recite a short version of the gospel, the New Tidings, he had memorized from Robinson. The full version, he told me, would take over two hours. Robert Goodvoice, an exceptionally intelligent, sensitive man with a gift for words, rendered the gospel into English for me to record as Mr. Two Bears gave it.

The recitation ended, the Douquettes and I, and my fast-asleep little boy, drove back through the dark pines to the North Saskatchewan River bridge and Prince Albert. I left them at their tent and parked the station wagon in the provincial campground near the river. If I were not a sober young mother with the warm reality of my little one always so close, I would have been sure I must have fantasized meeting followers of the Ghost Dance religion.

During the following days, I met the Douquettes again and returned to Round Plain, spending hours talking with Robert Goodvoice. Later, and through the following year, I visited the other Dakota reserves in Saskatchewan and several Plains Cree reserves to learn more of Indian religions in the province. At Moose Woods, I interviewed Fred Robinson's brother-in-law, a pillar of the Methodist mission there and a man who still strongly disapproved of his in-law always traipsing around to other reserves and neglecting to attend the Methodist church. At Standing Buffalo, I found a community that had kept the core of its Dakota religion without, it seemed, any need of revitalization through a movement such as the Ghost Dance. On the Cree reserve given to Poundmaker's band a century ago, I was privileged to talk for days with Piakwutch, maker of Sun Dances for all the reserves in the district, powerful healer, and model of selfless giving. Government banning of pagan rituals had driven Cree religion underground for years, but with increasing tolerance, Piakwutch had re-established its practice in his district.

My survey demonstrated that few Saskatchewan Indians had lost or rejected their peoples' religions, though many were members also of Christian churches (like Nick Black Elk). All the Indians in the southern (plains) section of the province had suffered the same severe deprivation as United States Plains Indians when the bison herds were exterminated in the 1880s. All the Saskatchewan Indian communities remained poor and subject to the Canadian version of the "Bureau Machine." In the 1930s, they had organized what eventually became, after thirty years of trials, the Federation of Saskatchewan Indians, often described as the most influential of the provincial Indian groups that formed the National Indian Brotherhood of Canada. No great religious movement has been recorded among Saskatchewan Indians. Have they directed revitalization into political channels?

An ethnohistorian can be content to delineate the complex narrative of Jack Wilson's Ghost Dance or of Saskatchewan Indians' histories. A few individuals stand out: Jack Wilson, Big Foot, John Tootoosis the dedicated political organizer from Poundmaker's band, Dennis Banks—whether good or bad, they stand out from the mass. The historian must look around and behind them to reveal the influences upon them, their heritages, the friends, followers, opponents, and events, large or local, that molded their achievements and fates. To assess the competing factors, historians need some educated sense of common patterns of human behavior.

Social scientists come in to offer hypotheses and descriptions of such patterns. Anthony Wallace's model of revitalization directs us to look for prophets offering new codes when times are badly out of joint. Framed by his model, Saskatchewan Indian ethnohistory seems to illustrate a political rather than religious movement in this century. The New Tidings was an exception to this, and it may be significant that it seems to have died, while Sioux Wahpeton Reserve, no longer usually called "Round Plain," has been led for years by an officer of the Federation of Saskatchewan Indians. Still, Indian religions remain strong in Saskatchewan, including at Sioux Wahpeton. The politicians, in strengthening the Indian communities, have strengthened the traditional religions. Elders, such as Joe and Florence Douquette now are, enjoy well-earned respect.

Jack Wilson's Ghost Dance was presented as a gospel, a message from God. Strengthening commitment to Indian religious beliefs, it strengthened the cohesiveness of Indian communities in the face of decades of efforts to disperse them. Contemporary Indian politicians sooner or later must touch base with their communities. Today, tribal community colleges teach both competency in dealing with the dominant society, and the language, beliefs, and legends of their peoples. Revitalization is strong, from multiplying Sun Dances on the Plains reservations, to a growing serious literature by self-consciously Indian authors. Religion and politics are aspects of the same tenacity in America's Indian nations.

When I wrote my doctoral dissertation for the professors at Harvard, I discussed Ralph Linton's four-cell matrix of types of "nativistic" movements, and Aberle's four-cells-plus-two, not to mention another anthropologist's four-stage model of American Indian "acculturation" that assumed the termination of the process to be assimilation into the marginal status in dominant American society. The neat pigeonholes looked conclusive: Jack Wilson, Fred Robinson, old Mr. Two Bears here, Piakwutch there, John Tootoosis the political organizer in another slot. The religious leaders all go into the "native-modified" box, John Tootoosis into "American-modified." Well, Tootoosis was more American-like than Piakwutch. Or was he? What about the occasion when Piakwutch, under his legal English name, gave the invocation at a Sports Day in the region's principal Euro-Canadian town? He spoke in Cree, of course, but as if he were the minister invited from a town church.

That night in Henry Two Bears' cabin wouldn't go into a pigeonhole. These were people, not "Indians." Their economic condition resulted from invasions, epidemics, international monopolies profiting from colonialism, railroad politics, world markets—the structure of Western capitalism as it emerged through four hundred years. Henry Two Bears' cabin wasn't "Indian," it was rural poverty. "Native-modified," "American-modified" involved economics. The Indians had not exterminated the bison herds; they had built them up over many centuries of managing the prairie ecosystem. Focusing on religious movements and military defeats reinforced the myth of the primitive laid upon the nations living on our continent when European capitalist policies and unchecked population growth leaped the ocean.

That night in the cabin, I realized how much my immigrant grandparents had been like contemporary American Indians. My grandparents had grown up pressured by the government of their country to use the dominant group's language, not that of their own people; to repudiate their religion and cultural traditions; to accept a marginal economic position, last hired, first fired, a life of poverty. My grandparents had escaped to America, losing their language but gaining security of income and religious expression, better health, opportunity for political influence. Where was "America" for American Indians? No other country welcomed them as immigrants, no other country promised them what their native land had denied them.

In recent years, anthropologists and other social scientists have increasingly realized how important, and how difficult, it is to resist innocently playing the tunes of ideology. Cold, hard, masculine objectivity wresting secrets from the bosom of Nature, or of natives, seduces its practitioners into manhandling data, stripping phenomena down to dead bits. We should not aim to construct a periodic table of the elements of humanity. James Mooney, conscious of his immigrant parents' suffering, could not deny his empathy with the people he talked with on Indian reservations. Mooney wrote ethnohistory and demonstrated that it could incubate social science so long as the comparisons were honest. No pigeonholes for Mooney's data: He told his readers, "The doctrines of the Hindu avatar, the Hebrew Messiah, the Christian millennium, and the Hesûnanin of the Indian Ghost Dance are essentially the same, and have their origin in a hope and longing common to all humanity" (Mooney [1896] 1973:657).

Jack Wilson was a Tövusi-dökadö doctor growing up on the American frontier. He dictated a letter to the President of the United States offering to manage affairs in the West, but the agent paid to assist the Paiute would not deign to send the letter. His offer ignored, Jack Wilson settled in to serve his own people and the hundreds who sought his inspiring wisdom. In South Dakota, the Lakota who were robbed of half their territory by the stroke of a pen in Washington protested to Congress. Their spokesmen were harassed, even shot, by local officials. Some Lakota, like Black Elk, traveled over half the world to find the best road for life, only to realize in old age that the revelation taught by the Lakota was as godly as any other people's. That message, an echo of Jack Wilson's, of Handsome Lake's, and of Tenskwatawa's, supports the resolve of American Indians today to continue the generations-long struggle for what, when you come right down to it, is America's classic promise—liberty and justice for all.

Why read about that Tövusi-dökadö in remote Mason Valley, Nevada, back in the nineteenth century? Why bother with those Indians taking over that hamlet of Wounded Knee in South Dakota? These are your fellow citizens, no vanishing race. And like any of us, they speak of "a hope and longing common to all humanity."

Sources

Chapter 1

Bailey, Paul, 1970.
Barney, Garold D., 1986.
Dangberg, Grace M., 1957.
D'Azevedo, Warren L., ed., 1986.
Kehoe, Alice Beck, field notes, Saskatchewan, 1961; 1962; 1973; 1984.
Lesser, Alexander, [1933] 1978.
Mooney, James, [1896] 1973.
Moses, L. G., 1984; 1985.
Siskin, Edgar E., 1983.

Chapter 2

Barney, Garold D., 1986.
Carlson, Leonard A., 1981.
Hoxie, Frederick E., 1984.
Johnson, W. Fletcher, 1891.
Knight, Oliver, 1960.
McLaughlin, James, [1910] 1970.
Milligan, Edward A., 1976.
Minneapolis Institute of Arts, 1976.
Mooney, James, [1896] 1973.
Powers, William K., 1977.
Prucha, Francis Paul, 1984.
Utley, Robert M., 1963.

Chapter 3

Bailey, Paul, 1970.
Barber, Bernard, 1941a.
Canfield, Gae Whitney, 1983.
Champagne, Duane, 1983.
Dangberg, Grace M., 1968.
Downs, James F., 1963.
Fleming, Paula Richardson and Judith Luskey, 1986.
Harmar, Nellie Shaw, 1974.
Hittman, Michael, 1971; 1973a; 1973b.
Jennings, Francis, 1975.
Johnson, Edward C., 1975.
Knack, Martha C. and Omer C. Stewart, 1984.
Lesser, Alexander, 1933; [1933] 1978.
Logan, Brad, 1980.

Mooney, James, [1896] 1973.
Moses, L. G., 1984; 1985.
Neihardt, John G., [1932] 1961; in DeMallie, 1984.
Prucha, Francis Paul, 1984.
Siskin, Edgar E., 1983.
Speth, Lembi Kongas, 1969.
Steward, Julian H., 1938.
Stewart, Omer C., 1977.
Wallace, Anthony F. C., 1956.
Whiting, Beatrice Blyth, 1950.
Wood, Neal, 1983; 1984.

Chapter 4

Dangberg, Grace M., 1957.
Frideres, James S., 1983.
Howard, James H., 1984.
Kehoe, Alice Beck, field notes, 1961; 1962; 1964; 1970; 1973; 1975; 1984.
Meyer, Roy W., 1968.
Perry, A. B., 1889.
Prucha, Francis Paul, 1984.
Saskatchewan Indian, 1984.

Chapter 5

Archambault, JoAllyn, personal communication, 1985; 1987.
Brown, Joseph Epes, 1953.
Castro, Michael, 1983 (chap. 3).
Deloria, Vine, Jr., 1979.
DeMallie, Raymond J., ed., 1984.
DeMallie, Raymond J. and Douglas R. Parks, eds., 1987.
Holler, Clyde, 1984.
Neihardt, John G., [1932] 1961.
Steinmetz, Paul B., 1980.

Chapter 6

Akwesasne Notes (publisher), 1974.
Archambault, JoAllyn, personal communication, 1985; 1987.
Carlson, Leonard A., 1981.
Day, Robert C., 1972.
Deloria, Vine, Jr., [1970] 1972.
Holm, Tom, 1981.
Iverson, Peter, 1982.
Jorgenson, Joseph G., 1978.
Mails, Thomas E., 1978; 1979.
Prucha, Francis Paul, 1984.
Talbot, Steve, 1978; 1981.
Vizenor, Gerald, 1984.
Walker, James R., 1982; 1983.
Weyler, Rex, 1982.

Chapter 7

Collins, June McCormick, 1974.
Frisch, Jack A., 1978.
Goldschmidt, Walter, ed., 1959.
Miller, Christopher L., 1985.
Mooney, James, [1896] 1973.
Morrison, Kenneth M., 1984.
Moses, L. G., 1984.
Ridington, Robin, n.d.; 1982.
Rybak, Boris, 1977.
Simmons, William S., 1979; 1983.
Spier, Leslie, 1935.
Stocking, George W., Jr., 1968.
Thurman, Melburn D. 1984; personal communication, 1985.
Walker, Deward E., Jr., 1969.

Chapter 8

Aberle, David F., 1959; 1962; 1966.
Brown, Kaye, 1976.
Carroll, Michael P., 1975.
Champagne, Duane, 1983.
Hill, W. W., 1944.
Landsman, Gail, 1979.
Mooney, James, [1896] 1973.
Moses, L. G., 1984.
Ortiz, Alfonso, ed., 1983.
Prucha, Francis Paul, 1984.
Spier, Leslie, Wayne Suttles, and Melville J. Herskovits, 1959.
Thornton, Russell, 1981; 1986.
Weiss, Lawrence David, 1984.
White, Richard, 1983.
Worsley, Peter, 1957.

Chapter 9

Barber, Bernard, 1941a; 1941b.
DeMallie, Raymond J. and Douglas R. Parks, eds., 1987.
Goldenweiser, Alexander, 1937.
Hittman, Michael, 1973a; 1973b.
Jennings, Francis, 1975.
Jennings, Francis, William N. Fenton, Mary A. Druke, and David R. Miller, eds.,
    1985.
Johansen, Bruce E., 1982.
La Barre, Weston, 1971; 1972.
Meek, Ronald L., 1976.
Mooney, James, [1896] 1973.
Morgan, Lewis Henry, [1851] 1954.
Sinte Gleska College, *Ahianpa*, 1987.
Trigger, Bruce G., ed., 1978.

Wallace, Anthony F. C., 1956; 1961; 1969.
Wood, Neal, 1983; 1984.

Chapter 10

Kehoe, Alice Beck, field notes, 1961; 1962; dissertation, 1964.
Mooney, James, [1896] 1973.

Recommended Reading

DeMallie, Raymond J., ed., 1984, *The Sixth Grandfather*. Lincoln: University of Nebraska Press.
    The texts of Neihardt's original interviews with Nick Black Elk, fully annotated and with a life of Black Elk by anthropologist DeMallie. If *Black Elk Speaks* is the "Bible" of Lakota religion, this is the original testament.

Hinsley, Curtis M., Jr., 1981, *Savages and Scientists*. Washington, DC: Smithsonian Institution Press.
    The formative years of the United States' premiere research institution, with special attention to the development of American ethnology.

Kehoe, Alice Beck, 1981, *North American Indians: A Comprehensive Account*. Englewood Cliffs, NJ: Prentice-Hall, Inc.
    The history of the American Indian nations, from first settlement of our continent thousands of years ago to contemporary political issues.

Mooney, James, [1896] 1973, *The Ghost-Dance Religion and Wounded Knee*. New York: Dover Publications, Inc.
    An inexpensive reissue in paperback of Mooney's masterpiece.

Bibliography

Aberle, David F.
  1959, The Prophet Dance and Reactions to White Contact. *Southwestern Journal of Anthropology* 15 (1):74–83.
  1962, A Note on Relative Deprivation Theory as Applied to Millenarian and Other Cult Movements. In *Millennial Dreams in Action*, ed. Sylvia L. Thrupp. Comparative Studies in Society and History, Supplement II, pp. 209–214. The Hague: Mouton & Co.
  1966, *The Peyote Religion Among the Navajo*. Viking Fund Publications in Anthropology, no. 42. New York: Wenner-Gren Foundation for Anthropological Research, Inc.

Akwesasne Notes
  1982, vol. 14, nos. 2, 3, 5; 1983, vol. 15, no. 5; 1984, vol. 16, nos. 3, 4, 5, 6. Rooseveltown, NY: Mohawk Nation at Akwesasne.

Akwesasne Notes (publisher)
  1974, *Voices from Wounded Knee, 1973*. Rooseveltown, NY: Mohawk Nation at Akwesasne.

Bailey, Paul
  1970, *Ghost Dance Messiah*. Los Angeles: Westernlore Press.

Barber, Bernard
  1941a, Acculturation and Messianic Movements. *American Sociological Review* 6:663–669.
  1941b, A Socio-Cultural Interpretation of the Peyote Cult. *American Anthropologist* n.s. 43(4): 673–675.

Barney, Garold D.
  1986, *Mormons, Indians and the Ghost Dance Religion of 1890*. Lanham, MD: University Press of America, Inc.

Barsh, Russel Lawrence and James Youngblood Henderson
  1980, *The Road*. Berkeley: University of California Press.

Berkhofer, Robert F.
  1978, *The White Man's Indian*. New York: Knopf.

Bowden, Henry Warner
  1981, *American Indians and Christian Missions*. Chicago: University of Chicago Press.

Boyd, Doug
  1974, *Rolling Thunder*. New York: Random House.

Brown, Joseph Epes
  1953, *The Sacred Pipe*. Norman: University of Oklahoma Press.

Brown, Kaye
   1976, Quantitative Testing and Revitalization Behavior: On Carroll's Explanation of the Ghost Dance. *American Sociological Review* 41:740–744.

Canfield, Gae Whitney
   1983, *Sarah Winnemucca of the Northern Paiutes*. Norman: University of Oklahoma Press.

Carlson, Leonard A.
   1981, *Indians, Bureaucrats, and Land*. Westport, CT: Greenwood Press.

Carroll, Michael P.
   1975, Revitalization Movements and Social Structure: Some Quantitative Tests. *American Sociological Review* 40:389–401. (See also his rejoinders, *American Sociological Review* 41:744–746; 44:166–168.)

Castro, Michael
   1983, *Interpreting the Indian*. Albuquerque: University of New Mexico Press.

Champagne, Duane
   1983, Social Structure, Revitalization Movements and State Building: Social Change in Four Native American Societies. *American Sociological Review* 48:754–763.

Collins, June McCormick
   1974, *Valley of the Spirits*. Seattle: University of Washington Press.

Dangberg, Grace M.
   1957, Letters to Jack Wilson, the Paiute Prophet, Written Between 1908 and 1911. Bureau of American Ethnology Anthropological Paper no. 55, Bulletin 164, pp. 279–296. Washington: Government Printing Office.
   1968, Wovoka. *Nevada Historical Society Quarterly* 11:1–53.

Day, Robert C.
   1972, The Emergence of Activism as a Social Movement. In *Native Americans Today: Sociological Perspectives*, ed. Howard M. Bahr, Bruce A. Chadwick, and Robert C. Day, pp. 506–532. New York: Harper & Row.

D'Azevedo, Warren L., ed.
   1986, *Handbook of North American Indians. Vol. 11, Great Basin*. Washington: Smithsonian Institution.

Deloria, Vine, Jr.
   [1970] 1972, This Country Was a Lot Better Off When the Indians Were Running It. In *Native Americans Today: Sociological Perspectives*, ed. Howard M. Bahr, Bruce A. Chadwick, and Robert C. Day, pp. 498–506. New York: Harper & Row.
   1974, *Behind the Trail of Broken Treaties*. New York: Dell Publishing Co.
   1979, Introduction. In *Black Elk Speaks*, John G. Neihardt, 1979 edition. Lincoln: University of Nebraska Press.

DeMallie, Raymond J.
   1978, Pine Ridge Economy: Cultural and Historical Perspectives. In *American Indian Economic Development*, ed. Sam Stanley, pp. 237–312. The Hague: Mouton & Co.
   ed., 1984, *The Sixth Grandfather*. Lincoln: University of Nebraska Press.

DeMallie, Raymond J. and Douglas R. Parks, eds.
   1987, *Sioux Indian Religion: Tradition and Innovation*. Norman: University of Oklahoma Press.

Doll, Don, and Jim Alinder
   1976, *Crying for a Vision*. Dobbs Ferry, NY: Morgan & Morgan.

Downs, James F.
   1963, Differential Response to White Contact: Paiute and Washo. University of Utah Anthropological Papers, no. 67:115–137.

Eastman, Elaine Goodale
   1945, The Ghost Dance War and Wounded Knee Massacre of 1890–91. *Nebraska History* 26(1):26–42.

Federation of Saskatchewan Indians (publishers)
   1982, *Saskatchewan Indian*. Vol. 12, no. 6. Prince Albert.

Fleming, Paula Richardson and Judith Luskey
   1986, *The North American Indians in Early Photographs*. New York: Harper & Row.

Fletcher, Alice C.
   1891, The Indian Messiah. *Journal of American Folklore* 4:57–60.

Frideres, James S.
   1983, *Native Peoples in Canada*, 2d ed. Scarborough: Prentice-Hall Canada, Inc.

Frisch, Jack A.
   1978, Iroquois in the West. In *Handbook of North American Indians*, Vol. 15, *Northeast*, ed. Bruce G. Trigger, pp. 544–546. Washington: Smithsonian Institution.

Gill, Sam
   1987, *Native American Religious Action: A Performance Approach to Religion*. Columbia: University of South Carolina Press.

Goldenweiser, Alexander
   1937, *Anthropology*. New York: F. S. Crofts and Co.

Goldschmidt, Walter, ed.
   1959, *The Anthropology of Franz Boas*. Memoir No. 89, American Anthropological Association. Menasha, WI: American Anthropological Association.

Grobsmith, Elizabeth
   1981, *Lakota of the Rosebud*. New York: Holt, Rinehart & Winston.

Harmar, Nellie Shaw
   1974, *Indians of Coo-yu-ee Pah (Pyramid Lake)*. Sparks, NV: Dave's Printing and Publishing.

Heidenreich, Charles Adrian
   1967, A Review of the Ghost Dance Religion of 1889–90 Among the North American Indians and Comparison of 8 Societies Which Accepted or Rejected the Dance. Master's thesis, University of Oregon, Eugene. (Manuscript in Heidenreich's possession.)

Hill, W. W.
   1944, The Navaho Indians and the Ghost Dance of 1890. *American Anthropologist* 46(4):523–527.

Hinsley, Curtis M., Jr.
   1981, *Savages and Scientists*. Washington: Smithsonian Institution Press.
   1985, Hemispheric Hegemony in Early American Anthropology, 1841–1851: Re-

flections on John Lloyd Stephens and Lewis Henry Morgan. In *Social Contexts of American Ethnology, 1840–1984*, ed. June Helm, pp. 28–40. Washington: American Ethnological Society.

Hittman, Michael
1971, The 1890 Ghost Dance Religion and Opiate Addiction Among Smith and Mason Valley Paiutes: Disillusionment or Retreatism? Paper presented at 70th Annual Meeting, American Anthropological Association, New York.
1973a, Ghost Dances, Disillusionment and Opiate Addiction: An Ethnohistory of Smith and Mason Valley Paiutes. Ph. D. diss., University of New Mexico, Albuquerque.
1973b, The 1870 Ghost Dance at the Walker River Reservation: A Reconstruction. *Ethnohistory* 20(3):247–278.

Holler, Clyde
1984, Black Elk's Relationship to Christianity. *American Indian Quarterly* 8(1): 37–49.

Holm, Tom
1981, Fighting a White Man's War: The Extent and Legacy of American Indian Participation in World War II. *Journal of Ethnic Studies* 9:69–81.

Howard, James H.
1984, *The Canadian Sioux*. Lincoln: University of Nebraska Press.

Hoxie, Frederick E.
1984, *A Final Promise: The Campaign to Assimilate the Indians, 1880–1920*. Lincoln: University of Nebraska Press.

Iverson, Peter
1982, *Carlos Montezuma*. Albuquerque: University of New Mexico Press.

Jennings, Francis
1975, *The Invasion of America*. New York: W. W. Norton.

Jennings, Francis, William N. Fenton, Mary A. Druke, and David R. Miller, eds.
1985, *The History and Culture of Iroquois Diplomacy*. Syracuse: Syracuse University Press.

Johansen, Bruce E.
1982, *Forgotten Founders*. Ipswich, MA: Gambit.

Johnson, Edward C.
1975, *Walker River Paiutes: A Tribal History*. Salt Lake City: University of Utah Printing Service.

Johnson, W. Fletcher
1891, *Life of Sitting Bull*. Philadelphia: Edgewood Publishing Co.

Jorgensen, Joseph G.
1978, A Century of Political Economic Effects on American Indian Society, 1880–1980. *Journal of Ethnic Studies* 6:1–82.

Kehoe, Alice Beck
1964, The Ghost Dance Religion in Saskatchewan, Canada. Ph. D. diss., Harvard University.
1970, The Dakotas in Saskatchewan. In *The Modern Sioux*, ed. Ethel Nurge, pp. 148–172. Lincoln: University of Nebraska Press.

1975, Dakota Indian Ethnicity in Saskatchewan. *Journal of Ethnic Studies* 3(2): 37–42.

1981, *North American Indians: A Comprehensive Account.* Englewood Cliffs, NJ: Prentice-Hall, Inc.

1985, The Ideological Paradigm in Traditional American Ethnology. In *Social Contexts of American Ethnology, 1840–1984*, ed. June Helm, pp. 41–49. Washington: American Ethnological Society.

Keller, Robert H., Jr.
1983, *American Protestantism and United States Indian Policy, 1869–82.* Lincoln: University of Nebraska Press.

Knack, Martha C. and Omer C. Stewart
1984, *As Long as the River Shall Run.* Berkeley: University of California Press.

Knight, Oliver
1960, *Following the Indian Wars.* Norman: University of Oklahoma Press.

La Barre, Weston
1971, Materials for a History of Studies of Crisis Cults: A Bibliographic Essay. *Current Anthropology* 12(1):3–44.

1972, *The Ghost Dance.* New York: Dell Publishing Co.

Landsman, Gail
1979, The Ghost Dance and the Policy of Land Allotment. *American Sociological Review*, 44:162–166.

Lesser, Alexander
1933, Cultural Significance of the Ghost Dance. *American Anthropologist* n.s. 35:108–115.

[1933] 1978, *The Pawnee Ghost Dance Hand Game.* Madison: University of Wisconsin Press. (Originally published as Columbia University Contributions to Anthropology, vol. XVI, New York.)

Linton, Ralph
[1943] 1971, Nativistic Movements. Reprinted in *Reader in Comparative Religion*, 3d ed., ed. William A. Lessa and Evon Z. Vogt, pp. 497–503. (Originally published in *American Anthropologist* 45:230–240.)

Logan, Brad
1980, The Ghost Dance Among the Paiute. *Ethnohistory* 27(3):267–288.

Mails, Thomas E.
1978, *Sundancing at Rosebud and Pine Ridge.* Sioux Falls, SD: The Center for Western Studies, Augustana College.

1979, *Fools Crow.* Garden City, NY: Doubleday.

Mason, W. Dale
1984, "You Can Only Kick So Long . . ." American Indian Movement Leadership in Nebraska 1971–1979. In *Indian Leadership*, ed. Walter Williams, pp. 21–31. Manhattan, KS: Sunflower University Press.

Matthiessen, Peter
1983, *In the Spirit of Crazy Horse.* New York: Viking Press.

1984, *Indian Country.* New York: Viking Press.

McLaughlin, James
   [1910] 1970, *My Friend the Indian*. Seattle: Superior Publishing Co. (Originally published by Houghton Mifflin, New York.)

Meek, Ronald L.
   1976, *Social Science and the Ignoble Savage*. Cambridge: Cambridge University Press.

Meyer, Roy W.
   1968, The Canadian Sioux, Refugees from Minnesota. *Minnesota History* 41(1): 13–28.

Miller, Christopher L.
   1985, *Prophetic Worlds*. New Brunswick, NJ: Rutgers University Press.

Miller, David Humphreys
   [1959] 1985, *Ghost Dance*. Lincoln: University of Nebraska Press.

Milligan, Edward A.
   1976, *Dakota Twilight*. Hicksville, NY: Exposition Press.

Minneapolis Institute of Arts
   1976, *I Wear the Morning Star*. Minneapolis: Minneapolis Institute of Arts. (No authors' names listed.)

Mooney, James
   [1896] 1973, *The Ghost-Dance Religion and Wounded Knee*. New York: Dover Publications, Inc. (Originally published as Part 2, *Fourteenth Annual Report 1892–93*, Bureau of Ethnology. Washington: Government Printing Office.)

Morgan, Lewis Henry
   [1851] 1954, *League of the Ho-de-no-sau-nee or Iroquois*, vol. 2. Reprinted by Human Relations Area Files, New Haven.

Morrison, Kenneth M.
   1984, *The Embattled Northeast*. Berkeley: University of California Press.

Moses, L. G.
   1984, *The Indian Man*. Urbana: University of Illinois Press.
   1985, "The Father Tells Me So!" Wovoka, the Ghost Dance Prophet. *American Indian Quarterly* 9(3):335–357.

Neihardt, John G.
   [1932] 1961, *Black Elk Speaks*. Lincoln: University of Nebraska Press. (Originally published by William Morrow and Company.) (See also under DeMallie, ed., 1984, *The Sixth Grandfather*, pp. 101–296.)

Newell, W. W., ed.
   1891, Account of the Northern Cheyennes Concerning the Messiah Superstition. *Journal of American Folklore* 4:61–69.

Ortiz, Alfonso, ed.
   1983, *Handbook of North American Indians*. Vol. 10, *Southwest*. Washington: Smithsonian Institution.

Ortiz, Roxanne Dunbar
   1980, Wounded Knee 1890 to Wounded Knee 1973: A Study in United States Colonialism. *Journal of Ethnic Studies* 8(2):1–15.

Overholt, Thomas W.
1974, The Ghost Dance of 1890 and the Nature of the Prophetic Process. *Ethnohistory* 21(1):37–63.
1978, Short Bull, Black Elk, Sword, and the "Meaning" of the Ghost Dance. *Religion* 8:171–195.

Perry, A. B.
1889, *Annual Report, 1888*. Appendix H, Report of the Commissioner of the North-West Mounted Police Force. Dominion of Canada Sessional Papers, vol. 13. Ottawa.

Phister, Nat P.
1891, The Indian Messiah. *American Anthropologist* 4(2):105–108.

Powers, Marla N.
1986, *Oglala Women*. Chicago: University of Chicago Press.

Powers, William K.
1977, *Oglala Religion*. Lincoln: University of Nebraska Press.

Prucha, Francis Paul
1984, *The Great Father*. Lincoln: University of Nebraska Press.

Ridington, Robin
n.d., From Hunt Chief to Prophet: Beaver Indian Dreamers and Christianity. Mimeographed paper in author's possession.
1982, Technology, World View and Adaptive Strategy in a Northern Hunting Society. *Canadian Review of Sociology and Anthropology* 19(4):469–481.

Rybak, Boris
1977, Une Convergence Remarquable Entre Langages Tambourinés, Codes Nerveux et Langages Machine. *L'Homme* XVII(1):117–121.

Saskatchewan Indian
1984, First Ministers' Conference—Analysis and Report. Special edition. Prince Albert: Federation of Saskatchewan Indians.

Sheehan, Bernard
1973, *Seeds of Extinction*. Chapel Hill: University of North Carolina Press.
1980, *Savagism and Civility*. Cambridge: Cambridge University Press.

Simmons, William S.
1979, Conversion from Indian to Puritan. *The New England Quarterly* 52(2):197–218.
1983, Red Yankees: Narragansett Conversion in the Great Awakening. *American Ethnologist* 10(2):253–271.

Sinte Gleska College
1987, *Ahianpa*. Vol. 1, no. 2, Rosebud, SD.

Siskin, Edgar E.
1983, *Washo Shamans and Peyotists*. Salt Lake City: University of Utah Press.

Speth, Lembi Kongas
1969, Possible Fishing Cliques Among the Northern Paiutes of the Walker River Reservation, Nevada. *Ethnohistory* 16(3):225–244.

Spier, Leslie
1935, *The Prophet Dance of the Northwest and Its Derivatives: The Source of the*

Ghost Dance. General Series in Anthropology, no. 1. Menasha, WI: George Banta Publishing Co.

Spier, Leslie, Wayne Suttles, and Melville J. Herskovits
    1959, Comment on Aberle's Thesis of Deprivation. *Southwestern Journal of Anthropology* 15(1):84–88.

Spindler, Will H.
    1972, *Tragedy Strikes at Wounded Knee.* Vermillion, SD: Dakota Press.

Steinmetz, Paul B.
    1980, *Pipe, Bible and Peyote Among the Oglala Lakota.* Stockholm: Almqvist & Wiksell International. (Acta Universitatis Stockholmiensis, Stockholm Studies in Comparative Religion 19.)

Steward, Julian H.
    1938, Basin-Plateau Aboriginal Sociopolitical Groups. Bureau of American Ethnology Bulletin 120. Washington: Government Printing Office.

Stewart, Omer C.
    1977, Contemporary Document on Wovoka (Jack Wilson), Prophet of the Ghost Dance in 1890. *Ethnohistory* 24(3):219–222.

Stocking, George W., Jr.
    1968, *Race, Culture, and Evolution.* New York: Free Press.

Stuart, Paul
    1981, The Christian Church and Indian Community Life. *Journal of Ethnic Studies* 9(3):47–55.

Talbot, Steve
    1978, Free Alcatraz: The Culture of Native American Liberation. *Journal of Ethnic Studies* 6(3):83–96.
    1981, *Roots of Oppression*, New York: International Publishers.

Thornton, Russell
    1981, Demographic Antecedents of a Revitalization Movement: Population Change, Population Size and the 1890 Ghost Dance. *American Sociological Review* 46:88–96.
    1986, *We Shall Live Again.* Cambridge: Cambridge University Press.

Thurman, Melburn D.
    1984, The Shawnee Prophet's Movement and the Origins of the Prophet Dance. *Current Anthropology* 25(4):530–531.

Trigger, Bruce G., ed.
    1978, *Handbook of North American Indians.* Vol. 15, *Northeast.* Washington: Smithsonian Institution.

U. S. Commission on Civil Rights, Staff Report
    1974, *Report of Investigation: Oglala Sioux Tribe, General Election, 1974.* Washington: U. S. Commission on Civil Rights.

Utley, Robert M.
    1963, *The Last Days of the Sioux Nation.* New Haven: Yale University Press.

Vizenor, Gerald
    1984, *The People Named the Chippewa.* Minneapolis: University of Minnesota Press.

Walker, Deward E., Jr.
  1969, New Light on the Prophet Dance Controversy. *Ethnohistory* 16(3):245–255.
Walker, James R.
  1982, *Lakota Society*. Ed. Raymond J. DeMallie. Lincoln: University of Nebraska Press.
  1983, *Lakota Myth*. Ed. Elaine A. Jahner. Lincoln: University of Nebraska Press.
Wallace, Anthony F. C.
  1956, Revitalization Movements: Some Theoretical Considerations for Their Comparative Study. *American Anthropologist* n.s. 58(2):264–281.
  1961, Cultural Composition of the Handsome Lake Religion. In *Symposium on Cherokee and Iroquois Culture*, ed. William N. Fenton and John Gulick, B.A.E. Bulletin 180, pp. 139–151. Washington: Smithsonian Institution.
  1969, *The Death and Rebirth of the Seneca*. New York: Random House.
Wassaja
  1983, vol. 10, no. 4. San Francisco: American Indian Historical Society.
Weiss, Lawrence David
  1984, *The Development of Capitalism in the Navajo Nation: A Political-Economic History*. Minneapolis: MEP Publications.
Weyler, Rex
  1982, *Blood of the Land*. New York: Random House. (Originally published by Everest House/Dodd, Mead & Company, Inc.)
White, Richard
  1983, *The Roots of Dependency*. Lincoln: University of Nebraska Press.
Whiting, Beatrice Blyth
  1950, *Paiute Sorcery*. Viking Fund Publications in Anthropology, no. 15. New York: Wenner-Gren Foundation for Anthropological Research, Inc.
Wissler, Clark
  1916, General Discussion of Shamanistic and Dancing Societies. American Museum of Natural History Anthropological Papers XI, pt. 12. New York.
Wood, Neal
  1983, *The Politics of Locke's Philosophy*. Berkeley: University of California Press.
  1984, *John Locke and Agrarian Capitalism*. Berkeley: University of California Press.
Worsley, Peter
  1957, *The Trumpet Shall Sound*. London: MacGibbon & Kee.
Zimmerman, Bill
  1976, *Airlift to Wounded Knee*. Chicago: Swallow Press.

Walker, Deward E., Jr.
1969, New Light on the Prophet Dance Controversy. *Ethnohistory* 16(3):245–255.

Walker, James R.
1982, *Lakota Society*. Ed. Raymond J. DeMallie. Lincoln: University of Nebraska Press.
1983, *Lakota Myth*. Ed. Elaine A. Jahner. Lincoln: University of Nebraska Press.

Wallace, Anthony F. C.
1956, Revitalization Movements: Some Theoretical Considerations for Their Comparative Study. *American Anthropologist* n.s. 58(2):264–281.
1961, Cultural Composition of the Handsome Lake Religion. In *Symposium on Cherokee and Iroquois Culture*, ed. William N. Fenton and John Gulick, B.A.E. Bulletin 180, pp. 139–151. Washington: Smithsonian Institution.
1969, *The Death and Rebirth of the Seneca*. New York: Random House.

Wassaja
1983, vol. 10, no. 4. San Francisco: American Indian Historical Society.

Weiss, Lawrence David
1984, *The Development of Capitalism in the Navajo Nation: A Political-Economic History*. Minneapolis: MEP Publications.

Weyler, Rex
1982, *Blood of the Land*. New York: Random House. (Originally published by Everest House/Dodd, Mead & Company, Inc.)

White, Richard
1983, *The Roots of Dependency*. Lincoln: University of Nebraska Press.

Whiting, Beatrice Blyth
1950, *Paiute Sorcery*. Viking Fund Publications in Anthropology, no. 15. New York: Wenner-Gren Foundation for Anthropological Research, Inc.

Wissler, Clark
1916, General Discussion of Shamanistic and Dancing Societies. American Museum of Natural History Anthropological Papers XI, pt. 12. New York.

Wood, Neal
1983, *The Politics of Locke's Philosophy*. Berkeley: University of California Press.
1984, *John Locke and Agrarian Capitalism*. Berkeley: University of California Press.

Worsley, Peter
1957, *The Trumpet Shall Sound*. London: MacGibbon & Kee.

Zimmerman, Bill
1976, *Airlift to Wounded Knee*. Chicago: Swallow Press.

Index

Aberle, David, 107–110, 125
Abernathy, Ralph, 82
Abourezk, James, 82, 86
Akwesasne Indian Nation, 53
Akwesasne Notes, 71, 80, 82–84, 88
Alcatraz Island, Indian occupation of, 53,
  75–76, 90, 127
Allegany Seneca Reservation, 116–117, 120
American Indian Chicago Conference, 74
American Indian Freedom of Religion Act,
  86
American Indian Movement (AIM), 48–
  49, 79, 90
  Alcatraz occupation and, 76
  birth of, 53, 71
  Indian Patrol of, 76
  in 1973 siege of Wounded Knee, 80–82,
    85–86, 89
  revitalization movement and, 125
  Trail of Broken Treaties and, 77, 81
American Revolution, 116
Aquash, Anna Mae, 85
Arapaho
  Ghost Dance practiced by, 8–9, 13–14
  Wilson's gospel brought to, 6–7, 35
Army, U.S., 19–21
  attempts to disarm Sioux by, 22–23
  war with Indians carried out by, 28–29
  in Wounded Knee massacre, 23–24
Assiniboin, 43–44
Augustine, St., 29

Bad Heart Bull, Amos, 78
Bad Heart Bull, Wesley, 78–79
Banks, Dennis, 76, 79, 81, 85, 125, 132
Barber, Bernard, 127, 131
Beaver, 99–100
Beecher, Henry Ward, 36, 38
Beecher, Lyman, 36
Bellecourt, Clyde, 76, 79, 125
Bellecourt, Vernon, 76, 125
Big Foot, 21–23, 38, 80–81, 84, 132
Bissonette, Gladys, 79
Black Coyote, 23–24
Black Elk, Anna, 64
Black Elk, Ben, 53–54, 56, 62, 65, 67
Black Elk, John, 62
Black Elk, Kate, 59, 62–64
Black Elk, Lucy, 62–66
Black Elk, Nicholas, 51, 79, 90–91, 102
  childhood visions of, 55–57

Christian conversion of, 62–69, 132
Ghost Dance practiced by, 38–39, 59
Iroquois religions and, 113
Neihardt's interview with, 53–54, 66–67,
  69, 78
on Oglala religion, 67–69
revitalization and, 123–125
ways of white man observed by, 57–59,
  134
Black Elk, Nicholas, Jr., 64
Black Elk Speaks (Neihardt), 51, 53–57,
  66–67, 76, 90
Black Hills Oglalas' claim to, 86–87
Black Road, 57
Blacksnake, 117, 121
Board of Trade, British, 126
Boas, Franz, 95–97
Bonnin, Zitkala-sa (Gertrude), 73
Brown, Dee, 80–81
Brown, Joseph Epes, 67–69, 102, 123
Buffalo, Sam, 44, 48
Buffalo Bill (William Frederick Cody), 18,
  20–21
  Wild West Show of, 21, 24, 55–56,
    57–59, 62
Bureau of Catholic Indian Missions, 66
Bureau of Indian Affairs (BIA), 19, 48, 53,
  67, 73–74, 77, 80–81, 83, 87, 91,
  107–108, 125, 132
Bury My Heart at Wounded Knee (Brown),
  80

Caddo, Ghost Dance practiced by, 8
California Gold Rush, 34
Camp Yellow Thunder, 86, 90
Canada
  Ghost Dance spread to, 44–48, 130–133
  Indian policy in, 48–50
  Sioux migration to, 41–43
Carlisle Indian School, 54, 65
Carroll, Michael, 105–106
Catches, Pete, 80
Catholic Indian Congress, 64–65
Census. U.S., 72
Cherokee, assimilation of, 28
Cheyenne, Wilson's gospel brought to, 6
Chicago, University of, 74
Chicago Herald, 19
Chippewa, 53
Civilian Conservation Corps (CCC), 73–74,
  108